THE EVENING GIRLS

Reflections of a District Nurse in the 1970s

ALICE WHITE

The Evening Girls

- *Reflections of a District Nurse in the 1970s*

ISBN: 978-1-7390972-4-0

Copyright © 2024 Alice White

All rights reserved. No parts of this publication may be reproduced, distributed, or transmitted in any form or by any means, including photocopying, recording, or other electronic or mechanical methods, without the prior written permission of the publisher, except in the case of brief quotations embodied in critical reviews and certain other noncommercial uses permitted by copyright law.

Published by Gossage Vears Publications, 2024

Edited by Siân-Elin Flint-Freel

Formatting and Cover design by Irish Ink Publishing

To Lesley, Lynn and Pauline – forever girls.
In memory of Vanessa.

District Nursing Reflections

- A STORY BEGINS

It was the 1970s. In a Midlands town, a dedicated team of district nurses – affectionately known as 'the evening girls' – worked tirelessly through the evening (often until midnight and beyond when things didn't go as planned) to provide nursing care to the local people in their own homes.

Today, nearly fifty years later, the remaining members of the team still meet as friends and reminisce about some of the homes they visited and their experiences with the unique individuals they encountered.

Seen through the eyes of Alice – the youngest of the evening girls – these stories are a glimpse into a bygone era of nursing, offering a humorous, moving and heart-warming look at the relationships between nurses and patients.

Although names and some details have been changed to protect the identity of those in the stories, these are true accounts – with as much accuracy as the evening girls' dwindling memories allow.

panic to locate the essential piece of paper with the list of tasks required, I somehow managed to tear and crumple up both sheets of the provided carbon paper required to make copies. Unable to complete the exam, it was effectively 'game over' for my secretarial aspirations.

The knowledge that a 'caring profession' would afford me some kudos in my family, which already boasted two great aunts who were nurses, and the fact I quite fancied the idea of wearing a uniform, was how I ended up becoming a cadet nurse at sixteen years old.

Part of the working week – including Saturdays – was spent gaining experience on the wards and departments of the local hospital. The remainder of my week was spent at college studying to gain the five 'O' levels required to be accepted at eighteen as a student on the three-year training course to qualify as a State Registered Nurse.

Known as pre-nursing students, in our pink linen dresses, crisp white aprons and impressively tall origami-like butterfly caps – although I never did quite master the art of folding mine correctly – I felt I'd found my vocation.

Mrs Hardy

- A STORY OF A DRAGON WITH A KIND HEART

"You don't lead by hitting people over the head – that's assault, not leadership."

Dwight Eisenhower

Previously, district nursing (now called community nursing) was funded and overseen by the local authority. In the 1970s, however, it moved under the control of the Health Authority, leading to many changes including the restructuring of nurse training and management, with District Nurses becoming 'attached' to GP Practices.

The Evening Nursing Service was a new development in our town. Prior to that, the District Nurses could be called out at any time of the night as well as in the day, especially to patients requiring terminal (end of life) care, and not too long before that, some of them also included midwifery in their role.

My three-year training towards becoming a registered nurse was cut short due to the birth of my first child, meaning that I had to settle for an Enrolled Nurse qualification — a more practical based role with, on completion, less managerial opportunities or responsibilities. Somehow, I felt like it was a lower status.

Later divorced and then with two young daughters, I took work in a shoe shop in the daytime as well as doing some extra work in care homes or any nursing agency work I could get to try to save enough for a deposit to buy us our own house. I had done a few shifts for the Marie Curie Night Sitting Nursing Service, and it was through that I heard there was a rare and much sought after vacancy 'on the district.'

This was even more appealing as it was evening work — just perfect to both fit around my children's needs and to earn some extra money. I would have to factor in the cost of a babysitter, but it would be easier to find one who would be available in the evenings. I applied and managed to secure an interview with the woman who I had heard was known as 'The Dragon'!

Mrs Hardy had been a district nurse for many years (perhaps even before I was born, or so I imagined as everyone over forty looks ancient when you are in your twenties). She had been promoted to a management role in the restructuring process, thus making her responsible for overseeing all the district nurses. She was hardcore and commanded attention — in an old-school hospital matronly way. Not a woman to mess with! It was immediately clear from the reception I received at my interview that she did not like me at all.

I had made so much effort focusing on my dress for the interview, ensuring my unruly hair was tied back, flat-heeled black shoes, white blouse buttoned up to the neck and calf-length black skirt, hoping to give the appearance of a sensible and responsible nurse. I had not, however, prepared myself with answers to any of the questions she fired at me at the speed of a machine gun.

She tutted when asking why I'd had my two children so young and questioned why I had not completed my training as a Registered Nurse. She doubted how I would manage if they were ill and I couldn't come to work. She asked me if I was planning on having more children and grilled me on what I would do if my car broke down.

It was only later, when I met the rest of the team and they relayed their experiences of her, that I realised I was not alone on her hit list – although it seemed she had a particular aversion to enrolled nurses.

I must have somehow bluffed my way through my answers because no-one was more surprised than me when she offered me the job. With at least three shifts a week, each 6.30pm-11pm, I was soon able to give up my work in the shoe shop. Well, actually, the manager there 'let me go' because I wasn't too good at selling shoes, being rather too honest when asked for my opinion by customers as to whether I thought their potential purchases suited them.

Two weeks after my interview, at 6.30pm sharp, I arrived at Mrs Hardy's house, absolutely terrified and certainly not relishing the idea of the final part of my initiation before I was let loose on my own – an evening round with Mrs Hardy.

My first mistake was unwittingly blocking her car in her driveway with my poor parking. She stood, hands on ample hips, and sighed wearily, watching me reverse, crunching the gears in my panic. A tall, sturdy woman, she had exchanged the tweed skirt and cashmere cardigan worn at my interview for a dark blue nursing matron's dress, her greying hair tucked securely under her navy pill box hat. I felt positively scruffy when I saw her, even though I had made my very best effort in my well-ironed dark green uniform dress on which I proudly displayed my badge of qualification along with the fob watch – a present for passing my nursing exams from my delighted father.

She had to unbuckle the silver clasp on her belt in order to miraculously manage to squeeze herself into the driver's seat of her very small Austin Mini car, throwing her nursing bag with gusto onto the back seat. I noted her belt buckle depicted George and the dragon and wondered if that's where her nickname had come from. Meanwhile, I slid into the passenger seat, immediately needing to steady myself with my hand on the dashboard as she drove like a tyrant, completely indifferent to any other drivers on the road, glaring at them as they dispersed in all directions to avoid her. No seat belt laws in those days.

By the time we arrived at our first patient's house I was just pleased to still be in one piece, only now feeling safe to open my eyes after closing them following a particularly harrowing experience when she drove straight across a crossroads with her hand on the horn, narrowly missing a cyclist. The patient's wife opened the door and when she saw Mrs Hardy she almost curtseyed as if she was welcoming the Queen. She fussed around, apologising for the state of her house while Mrs Hardy bustled around her anxious looking husband, and if he could have got up from his wheelchair, I think he would have stood to attention and saluted.

In fact, all the patients we visited that first night – and I can't say I remember who they were as it was all a bit of a blur – seemed in awe of her. She seemed to hold an air of efficiency in her work but without much time for chatting or compassion for them. However, I heard a surprising story from one man as we talked in the kitchen while Mrs

Hardy was washing her hands in the bathroom. His elderly mother had needed to move to a sheltered housing complex but couldn't afford the removal costs. Unphased by the challenge, Mrs Hardy had borrowed a pick-up truck, loaded it with the woman's furniture, and delivered it all to her new home, along with the woman perched in her armchair like a queen on the throne on the back of the truck. After hearing this story, it was easier and quite encouraging to see that under her brusque exterior there may have been a kind heart – although she never revealed it to me.

So, it came about that I survived that night and another twenty or so years as the youngest of the evening girls – and the only one wearing a green uniform dress instead of the blue of the registered nurses.

Mrs Hardy had a point with her concerns about childcare. Most of the time it worked out well and my two daughters either stayed with their dad when I was working, or with the willing and very capable teenager, Angela, who was always up for some extra pocket money.

However, there were times when it was not so easy, such as the time I got a phone call from Angela to say she had been held up at college and would be late. I had no option but to bundle my girls into the back of the car to go to base and collect my list of patients for the evening and then return home to drop them off, hopefully when Angela would have arrived. This shouldn't have been too much of a problem, but when I arrived in the car park at base I was horrified to see the familiar green mini, and worse than that, Mrs Hardy was in the process of shoehorning herself out of it, paying one of her impromptu visits to check up on us!

"Get down!" I hissed at my daughters, who were always up for playing a game, but it seemed not this time – they must have sensed my anxiety.

"Why?" they protested.

"We're just going to play hide and seek with the lady. Stay down while I go into the office. I won't be long."

As I got out, to my relief they ducked down just as Mrs Hardy glanced over towards my car. I thought I'd got away with it until…

"Nurse – what colour tights are you wearing?" her voice boomed.

I had struggled to find a pair without a hole in but I didn't think they were that far from the regulation uniform tan shade we were supposed to wear.

"Take them off NOW and go and find a pair in the correct colour."

I was shaken for a minute and then realised she actually did mean 'NOW', so in the middle of the car park she stood watching me wriggle out of my tights! Luckily, I was going home to drop off the girls so I could find some more but I decided not to mention that.

In those pre-email and mobile phone days, it was not unusual to find a note in our pigeonholes. The little wooden compartments that lined the left-hand wall of the office base, each with our names sellotaped on, were our way of communicating with one another or the day nurses. We all got on well and sharing laughter was one of the ways we coped with both the wrath of Mrs Hardy and the sometimes difficult job we were doing. One of the day nurses who had a particularly dry sense of humour, on hearing of my encounter in the car park, used to leave me amusing little notes and poems:

'Dear Nurse, You have been chosen to perform an additional duty – that of ensuring all staff are wearing the correct colour tights. You

will be present in the car park at the start of shifts to perform full leg inspections and will be held fully accountable for any nurse who does not comply.'

The office at that time was based in the grounds of the then geriatric hospital, which originally, many years earlier, had been the workhouse and it still bore the bleakness and a few rumours of ghosts from that time. As a cadet, I had served a three-month placement on the wards there with two hours at the end of each week spent sitting at a dusty desk poring over a huge leather-bound book, recording by hand the notes the ward staff had left, with that week's information on admissions, discharges and deaths. I found it a fascinating task and I often wonder what happened to all those records when the hospital closed in 1993 and geriatric patients were moved to the general wards of the main hospitals and no longer segregated. There were four wards on the ground floor of this dark, gloomy building. Up the narrow stone steps was Ward 5 – the 'long-stay' ward. It was unspoken but everyone knew patients were never discharged from this ward and the only entries in the book from there went in the 'deaths column'.

The messages we nurses dreaded seeing in our pigeonholes were those written in red biro – knowing they would be from Mrs Hardy. The following Friday evening following my clash with her in the car park, it was my turn to receive the poison-pen letter. My hands shook slightly as I opened the piece of paper and "SEE ME!" jumped out at me from the page. Thus followed a very anxious weekend wondering what on earth I could have done wrong.

When I plucked up the courage to go into Mrs Hardy's office at nine o'clock on Monday morning, I had convinced myself I was – at best – going to be dismissed. I knocked on the door of her office and, receiving no reply, I cautiously entered, hoping against hope she wasn't there. However, she was standing in the far corner of the room in front of a tall, open cupboard. She turned around suddenly as if surprised to see me and then lurched backwards a little, almost falling before regaining her balance.

"Yes – what is it, nurse?"

"You wanted to see me, Mrs Hardy – you left me a note?"

"Did I? I don't remember."

Still looking flustered, she slammed the door of the cupboard shut and I was sure I spotted a large bottle of gin on the top shelf before, with a flapping of her hands, she waved me away as if I was an annoying insect that was hovering around her head.

She never spoke of our meeting again.

Sacrifice

'Perhaps one day, they'll understand all the sacrifices she gladly made out of love for them.'

John Mark Green

'The reasons women from older generations often seem to put the needs of others before their own are complex. We all complain from time to time how hard life can be, but witnessing these sacrifices firsthand was a powerful reminder of the strength and compassion found in these women. Here are the stories of two strong women we met on our visits.'

Miss Johnson

- A STORY OF LOSS AND LONELINESS

"Good evening, Miss Johnson."

My attempt at a cheery voice echoed around the huge dark musty-smelling kitchen which also served as a living area. (My strict nurse training had taught me never to call a patient by their first name unless they requested it, on the premise that people, especially those of a certain age, might find it disrespectful). In fact, everyone in the village where Miss Johnson lived, just on the outskirts of the small town, had only ever known her as Miss Johnson, and her beloved pet bird as 'that bloody parrot.'

My jovial voice was somewhat false that night. It had already been a very long evening with several extra visits squeezed in at the last minute added to my already bulging list. It wasn't helped by a protracted wait for an on-call GP to visit a patient who I'd suspected would need admission to hospital. The GP had sounded quite grumpy on the phone, leaving me thinking he didn't want to leave his fireside on such a cold and gloomy October night any more than I did.

With a heavy heart, I could think of little else than my

own cosy bed while knowing from experience that this visit to help the somewhat uncooperative Miss Johnson to her bed and settle her for the night was not going to be quick. It was already 10.30 p.m. and there were still two more patients to visit on the other side of town.

Taking off my navy thick tweed winter uniform coat, and carefully folding it outside in – another useful tip taught in my training to prevent transferring any potential infections from one house to another – I winced on hearing, "What's good about it? You're late." The crackly, weak voice coming from the darkest corner of the kitchen grated on me as I lay my coat over the back of the rickety wooden chair in the other corner – the cleanest spot I could find in the dusty space. Taking a deep breath in preparation, I took my freshly laundered white tabard out of my nursing bag and slipped it over my head, fastening the two buttons at the side.

Looking over at her frail hunched body slumped in the worn armchair by the gas fire – the only modern convenience in the ancient cottage – it was impossible not to account for how her hard life had taken its toll on her health. She was relatively young compared to some of our other patients but being ridden with arthritis had left her looking much smaller than her actual height of around five foot seven and much older than her seventy-six years.

Beyond her cantankerous exterior was a strong woman – as many of her generation were forced to be – only now getting the care she had been denied throughout her own childhood. Instead she had devotedly sacrificed her own needs to care for others. It was difficult not to feel compassion for her, and while feeling a little ashamed of my impatience at the same time, I still didn't relish the lengthy visit I knew this would be.

There was no hurrying Miss Johnson.

So, changing tack and trying to jolly her along a little, with a smile, I offered, "Would you like a drop of whiskey in your hot milk tonight – warm you up a bit?"

Clearly wasted on her, my effort was rejected as defiantly as a cat spitting out a worm tablet. (If you've ever tried this impossible manoeuvre, you'll know what I mean).

"You know I never touch it," she almost snarled as she reached down into the side of the cushion of her armchair, her gnarled hands pulling out the tattered sepia photo, the one I'd seen so many times. A more wistful voice now, and wiping a tear from her cheek with a grubby looking man's hanky pulled from the sleeve of her powder blue crocheted bedjacket: "Did I tell you my Albert loved a wee drop?"

I hoped she hadn't heard my (rather too loud) sigh while I stooped to take the small, battered aluminium milk pan concealed behind the flowery cotton curtain under the big Belfast sink. I poured milk from the glass bottle, knowing from many weary nights of experience exactly how much would be needed to fill the Thermos flask which saw her through the night, and replaced the tea in the other flask left by the Home Help every afternoon.

As I lit the ring on the ceramic gas stove, I remembered my first week in the job during the exceptionally hot summer when I thought I would be helpful in suggesting to her she might need a fridge to stop the milk from going sour in the heat.

"That's what your nose is for, nurse, not for poking it into other folk's business!"

So, no matter what the season, the milk bottles were preserved in the stainless steel bucket half full of cold (or sometimes turned lukewarm) water, leaving me well and truly reprimanded and learning a sharp lesson – nursing a patient in their own home was going to be very different to hospital nursing where patients tended to comply and do as they were instructed.

Glancing across to the other corner of the room at (parrot) Albert's cage, I was half hopeful he may be settled in there already, but seeing how the evening was going, I knew there was not a chance of this and his capture would have to come later.

Whilst I waited for the milk to heat my mind wandered to piecing together – from the stories she told us when in a more talkative mood – the picture of the young Margaret Johnson and the sadness, loss and hardship that she had endured for most of her life.

First her beloved father was tragically killed in a horrific altercation with a tractor on the small farm which stood on this spot – now long gone, this tiny house being her only inheritance and a reminder of her early family life.

Shortly after her father's death, her mother took to her bed, giving up the management of both the other workers on the farm and the additional sewing work she took in to supplement the family's sparse income. It was from that day she also gave up care of her four daughters – her 'illness' would nowadays be understood as a deep and intractable depression.

Just thirteen years old, Margaret had taken on responsibility for the care of not only her mother, but her three sisters, aged eleven, nine and eight. (Two of the sisters were long gone now – not from neglect on Margaret's part.) Even with her best efforts, she could not provide adequately for the health of this already impoverished family that now lacked a wage earner.

The youngest, Sally, only survived her father by a year – her death compounding her mother's already broken heart. She didn't have the resistance to fight the diphtheria

– a deadly illness then, long before vaccinations became available in the 1940s.

Oldest of the three, Elizabeth, was taken in childbirth, along with her child conceived out of wedlock from a brief encounter with the only remaining farm hand, George, who promptly disappeared when the sixteen-year-old Elizabeth, with her bulging belly, could conceal her shame no longer.

Miss Johnson talked often and fondly about these two cherished sisters and still, even after all these years, held onto much anger towards George.

Her other sister, Vera, fared much better. Along with her husband, Tom, and their two young children, she was one of the million or so '£10 Poms' leaving the UK for a better life in Australia after the Second World War, assisted by the Australian government Migration Scheme. They kept in touch with Margaret for a while but feared having too much to do with her in case she called on them to assist with looking after their ailing and increasingly difficult mother.

By the time Mother died in 1965, it was deemed 'too much water had flowed under the bridge' to resume contact and the rift grew between them. They didn't attend Mother's funeral and I imagined there was more than a little jealousy on Margaret's part, having given up most of her life to care for Mother, and indeed her early life caring for the sister that now had 'abandoned' her.

They were happy to 'allow' Margaret to keep their potential share of their inheritance, which basically amounted to the run-down house. They'd settled well in Australia, and as Margaret had to acknowledge, 'that was the end of that.'

Albert – Margaret's only real chance of escape to freedom – had just missed avoiding conscription to fight in the Second World War at the age of forty-nine and sadly lost his life while a prisoner of war in Japan just before his potential repatriation at the end of the conflicts. Her affections for Albert were now immortalised in her beloved parrot of the same name.

"Nurse, mind you don't boil it. You'll take all the goodness out of it!"

Jolted out of my musings, I resisted saying there's little fear of boiling the milk even if I stayed there all night with the pathetically low gas flame that spluttered and spat. Instead, trying to summon up as much kindly patience as I could, aware that if she sensed my irritation it would only slow her down more, I replied, "It's fine, Miss Johnson, I've never spoiled it yet, have I? Come on, let's get you into bed before it's time to get up again."

"You're always in such a hurry, you nurses. I've not even finished my drink yet."

She reached out her trembling hands and unscrewed the top of the afternoon thermos flask, shaking out the last remaining dregs of tea into the slightly chipped blue willow patterned teacup that sat expectantly on the faded lilac-painted table by her chair.

Hopeful of some inspiration but without much optimism on how to speed up the proceedings, I asked, "Is Albert ready for bed? Could you ask him to get into his cage?"

Miss Johnson groaned as she reached for a very long cane from behind her chair, retrieving it like an arrow from a quiver, and after a few frustrating (for me) attempts, adeptly flicked up the catch of Albert's cage, thus opening the door. In a tired voice, she called him. The almost featherless, scruffy-looking Albert responded by appearing from his dark corner, flying around my head a couple of times, causing me to duck down in fear before swooping into his cage with an evil sounding cackly laugh. Miss Johnson swiftly nudged the cage door shut with a satisfied smile.

Composing myself, I manage a (through gritted teeth) "Thank you".

"Now let's get you tucked up."

"You haven't done my hair yet, nurse," she said, holding out a comb she had drawn from the fabric bag she kept down the other side of her chair.

As gently as I could, I teased the comb through the few wispy strands that remained on her aged head, trying to imagine her as a young girl with beautiful flowing locks. I felt slightly guilty when thinking how much, as a child, I hated my own curly mass of red hair. It must be the worst thing as a woman to lose your hair.

Miss Johnson seemed brighter and was slowly sipping her drink.

"Have you found any nits, nurse?" encouraged me to join in the banter and pretend to find one of the unwanted lively visitors, but Miss Johnson had moved on and was already reminiscing again.

"I used to check the girls' heads every night..." Her voice tailed off as she looked vacantly out of the window into the darkness.

"I'm sure you did a great job looking after them."

But this comment seemed inadequate to jog her out of her memories and bring her back to the job in hand. She started to shuffle towards the front of her chair, her joints creaking painfully. She had become impatient.

"C'mon then, nurse, let me get to bed. I can't sit here all night talking to you."

There was no need to change her into night clothes as she rarely wore anything but her nightdress and bedjacket, aside from when the ambulance came to take her to hospital outpatient visits, which according to her were, "A waste of bloody time." We had to agree on this; no-one, not even the smartest doctors, could help ease her pain very much – neither the physical nor emotional.

She held out cupped hands for her night-time medication and bent her head lower to take the pills to her mouth, swallowing them in one go with the glass of water I held for her.

Then began the long journey to the front sitting room of the house which had, for many years, since she became unable to get up the stairs, been her bedroom. None of the nurses had ever seen the upstairs rooms, so could only imagine what treasures might be hidden there.

Walking behind to steady her as she shuffled along with her walking frame half an inch at a time, eventually we arrived, and I supported her to lower onto the commode before returning to the kitchen to give her some privacy.

Realising I hadn't put any seed in the cage for Albert, I grabbed a handful from the rusty Ovaltine tin and noted to my horror the cage door was open and he was gone! It was getting late and I couldn't help thinking that Miss Johnson deliberately hadn't dropped the catch properly – another ploy to keep me there longer. Fortunately, throwing the seed into the cage and a few choice words from me bribed Albert out from the corner of the room. He hesitated a little by my ankles, where he took a last feeble attempt at a peck, before hovering around a bit and finally hopping into his cage.

Shutting the door of the cage and covering it with a towel before the crafty bird could escape again, I uttered a curt, "Goodnight, Albert".

On my return to the bedroom, Miss Johnson was trying to get to her feet. I helped her to turn around so her back was against the side of the huge feather bed, which took up the best part of the small room – the same bed that her mother inhabited for her final years. The next part of the operation was lengthy and precise as she wriggled and squirmed, twisted and turned, rocking from side to side – each wriggle moving her bottom further and further into the deep feather mattress. A muffled "Ready!" and I quickly and gently lifted her stiff joint-locked legs around and onto the bed. More shuffling and snuggling ensued until she finally almost disappeared into the deep marshmallow of a mattress, only her nose peeped out over the edge of the faded pink satin eiderdown that gave her frail body some extra warmth.

So, an hour and ten minutes exactly – no more, no less, as always – I set off on my way to my next patient's house, wondering what it must be like to be that lonely and musing on what an awfully long time parrots can live.

Marge

- A STORY OF STRENGTH, DEVOTION AND HARD WORK

Most people visiting the town's oldest pub down by the canal were looking to enjoy a drink or a game of dominoes. Our evening visits to The Angler's Retreat, however, were for a less pleasurable reason.

It was striking when walking in from the evening summer sunshine – the smoky darkness of the bar in contrast to the far end of the room where a beam of sun gleamed like a spotlight silhouetting two men still in work clothes sitting at a table with their heads close together deep in conversation.

Some pubs in the town were just beginning to serve full meals. However, in The Fishers – as it was affectionately known by its regulars – there was nothing tastier on offer other than the strange sight of clutches of pickled eggs floating in two huge jars placed at either end of the dark highly polished mahogany bar. The only exception was on Tuesday's 'darts nights' when landlady Marge would bring out a veritable feast on huge china serving platters. According to Marge, the china had belonged to Jack's (her husband's) mother. It would be piled high with egg and cress, cheese, ham and roast beef sandwiches followed by another platter, on which was a perilously balancing tower of homemade hot sausage rolls. At Christmastime, mince pies would be a tasty addition made from Marge's 'secret' recipe, laced with – for those who were brave enough to try them – an eye-watering amount of brandy.

I spotted Marge, a plump homely looking woman in her seventies, behind the bar as always in her blue forties-style flowery wrap-around apron, one hand resting on the tall vintage brass-topped beer pump, the other on her ample hip. She always looked exhausted – unsurprisingly with the long hours she worked. Singlehandedly running the pub from eleven in the morning until three in the afternoon with only a short break in which she would cycle up the hill into the town to visit the home of her elderly mother, prepare her tea and tidy the house, and then back to work from six till eleven in the evening. The only brief respite being on Sundays when the licensing hours meant she could close at 10.30 p.m. but even at that late hour she still had the tables to clear and the glasses to wash.

Her husband of fifty years, Jack, on the other hand, led a much easier life, having not actually worked in the pub for many years. No-one seemed to know for certain why he had retired early, but rumour had it some sort of 'accident' had occurred and apparently Jack had 'never been the same since.' He did, however, play the host very well and he was almost a permanent fixture to be found leaning at the end of the bar with a pint in his hand chatting to one of the locals.

Marge was very loyal and hardly ever complained about Jack's lack of support, even when she had to go down to the cellar and change the heavy barrels. I imagined this task, along with pulling all those pints, was why, although she had very muscular arms, years of relentless hard work had taken its toll, weakening the rest of her body. This was why the daytime nurses had requested a second visit from us in the evening to change the dressings on her badly ulcerated legs. Even though the whole team did their best, we all agreed our combined efforts on these twice daily visits were probably in vain as her legs were unlikely ever to heal permanently due to the hours she spent standing on them.

Marge saw me standing in the doorway, my eyes still attempting to adjust to the gloominess, and I jumped when I heard her assert herself. Even though Jack's name as licensee was above the door, it was clear who was the real boss here.

"JAAACK!" Marge shouted sharply across the bar. "Nurse is here. C'mon, stop your wittering and get over here and do some work for a change!"

Jack, a tiny whippet of a man and a good six inches shorter than Marge, obediently put down his drink and trotted quickly across to stand beside her.

Then more softly and with a resigned half smile to me, she said, "Hello nurse, how are you? We need to keep the men in check, don't we? He'll be the death of me, that man."

I smiled to myself, picturing this otherwise homely looking woman throwing out a rowdy customer or two, holding them aloft by their pants, legs dangling in the air.

As I wove my way towards the bar through the (all male) patrons, I felt a little self-conscious of their stares and looked straight ahead, trying to hide my discomfort and adopt a professional air to focus on the job in hand. Marge lifted the hinged bar flap, and we walked along a narrow passageway to the back of the pub and into the kitchen, come living room, come storeroom, come office.

Newspapers were piled high in one corner and what

looked like —- from the buff-coloured envelopes – a stack of bills in another. Two elastic stockings, a badly stained crepe bandage and a pair of incontinence pants were hanging to dry on a metal fireguard in front of a small paraffin heater. The combination of the stench of ammonia from the pants and the fumes from the heater caused me to catch my breath. The rest of the room was crammed full of all sorts of junk: boxes overflowing with clothes, stacks of books, some old brewery display boards, a bright yellow Schweppes ice bucket, a couple of jars of pickled onions and a little yellow figurine with a blue bow which I recognised from TV adverts in my childhood as the Babycham deer. There was hardly an area of the threadbare carpet left uncovered.

Marge collapsed into her armchair with a sigh of relief in anticipation of a few minutes' break. I hung my coat on one of the bright orange knobs of the modern tubular metal coat stand which looked strangely out of place and not in keeping with the rest of the 1940s décor and moved towards the sink to wash my hands, having first removed the big fluffy tabby cat who had taken up permanent residence there amongst the stack of dirty dishes.

Grateful that I carried my own hand towel as there didn't seem to be a clean one available to use, it took a few minutes to locate the cardboard box that contained the dressings and I eventually found it under a moth-eaten brown blanket on the top of the chest freezer. I cleared as much space as possible before opening the box on the table beside Marge's chair. Laying out a piece of newspaper over the little tapestry footstool, I covered it with a sterile paper towel from a dressing pack, and helped Marge lift her heavy bandage-laden leg onto it to support her throughout the half hour long process of changing her dressings.

Starting to unwrap the first layer of bandage, it was

noticeable that a lot of fluid from the ulcers had seeped through and dried hard, causing the layers below to stick. Even trying to be as gentle as possible and soaking off the crusted dressings with saline from a syringe, Marge still winced in pain as I worked to remove them.

"You must try and rest your legs up when you can," I suggested, knowing that with her life the way it was, selflessly she would not comply.

She confirmed my fears with a resigned, "Fat chance of that, nurse. Who is going to run this place? Not Jack, that's for sure, with his nerves so bad since his accident."

I tried to keep the conversation light-hearted, knowing how much Marge valued our nursing visits. Her legs began to shrink considerably with the removal of each layer. Gingerly, I lifted the final piece of gauze and was just about to give in to my curiosity and ask more about Jack's accident when … I could hardly believe what I was seeing. To my horror, the deep ulcer on Marge's leg was alive with a mass of wriggling hungry maggots! I quickly grabbed a fresh piece of gauze to cover the crime scene before Marge noticed – unable to stop myself shuddering, although trying to compose myself.

"How's it doing, nurse? It's been very itchy recently. They say that's a sign it's getting better?" Marge asked, giving me a hopeful look.

I managed to scoop up a couple of maggots that I noticed had absconded onto the carpet, using a disposable plastic glove, quickly turning it inside out and hoping that Marge's eyesight was not good enough to spot them.

"Not too bad," I lied, "though I think it might be time to have a word with your day nurse to see if she wants to change your treatment."

Marge nodded. "I'll leave it up to you, nurse. You know what you're doing."

I actually didn't, but I carried on regardless, cleaning the ulcer by syringing on more saline solution than usual, watching carefully to ensure the very last little creature was flushed into the paper towel. Once it was clear of 'guests', surprisingly the ulcer did seem to be looking quite healthy – much better than it had last time I had seen it.

Opening a brown glass bottle cautiously, I poured some Gentian Violet – an antiseptic lotion – into the little plastic pot taken from the dressing pack, obsessively checking three times that the cap of the bottle was tight, not wanting to repeat a horrific experience my colleagues were quick to tell me about on my first day. The story goes that one of the daytime district nurses had not been so careful and while rather vigorously shaking the bottle spilt the entire contents of the deep violet indelible liquid on a patient's plush cream coloured carpet.

Continuing to rebuild the layers of gauze and bandages, I applied the final crepe bandage and Marge's leg again reached double the size of her 'good leg'. I didn't see any point in telling her about my unexpected find, and in any case, I was still battling with my own queasy feeling.

"Thank you, nurse. It's always good to see you. Back to work now," she said wearily.

I wrapped all the dirty dressings tightly in the newspaper, disposing of them into an old carrier bag taken from a pile on the floor and then into another just in case. The whole lot went into a yellow clinical waste bag which was collected once a week by the local council, by which time I was hopeful, devoid of their 'lunch' from Marge's leg, the intruders would have starved to death.

Washing my hands, I made a mental note to leave a message for Marge's day nurse about my experience.

With my back turned as Marge took her last few minutes of rest, she called out, "Oooh, I nearly forgot, nurse, there's some freshly baked cheese scones in the oven. Would you like to take a couple home for your supper? I know they are your favourite."

For no other reason (of course), reflecting that sometimes the most important part of the home visit is not the treatment but the company, and knowing how offended Marge would be if I'd refused, I thanked her, and taking the paper bag with the still warm scones, I tried not to think too much about the hygiene standards in Marge's kitchen. After all, they were the very best cheese scones I've ever tasted.

First Impressions

'Don't judge a book by its cover.'

George Eliot

'We all make assumptions and judgements which come from our diverse personal experiences – past and present. Two very different stories here which show first impressions aren't always accurate.'

The Major

All the nurses agreed a visit to the Major was like entering into another world – a home that was a complete contrast to Miss Johnson's modest dwelling.

Waiting in the magnificent porch after a tug on the traditional doorbell, I always felt a little like a servant who had forgotten her key. After a few minutes, I heard a couple of internal doors open and close, followed by the sound of high-pitched yelping increasing in volume as the creature responsible neared the front door. A clip clop of heels on the marble floor and then the familiar quiet but slightly ruffled sounding woman's voice: "Quiet, Winston! He won't hurt you, nurse, he's just a little grumpy this evening."

Hearing the clipped tones of her fake upper-class accent, my mother's voice resounded in my head: "Sounds like she is talking with a plum in her mouth."

I tried adopting a more serious expression on hearing much clanking of locks and bolts and prepared to greet the 'lady of the house' – the Major's wife, Mrs Kilpatrick – who eventually appeared in the open doorway holding what can only be described as a small white pig with black markings over one ear.

A slight woman, no more than five feet two tall, Mrs Kilpatrick's silver hair was tied back tightly in a bun secured with a black velvet ribbon, only a couple of flustered strands escaping onto her forehead as she clearly battled with the wriggling 'piglet' who was trying to escape from under her arm.

"It's OK, you can put Winston down if you wish, I know he won't bite."

With a small sigh of relief, she placed him on the floor and made several sweeping gestures to smooth her dark green tweed skirt, patting her throat and fussily stroking the string of pearls that sat just above the slightly off-white frilled collar of her blouse.

At a recent team meeting we had taken bets on Winston's breed – once we had finally come to the conclusion he was in fact a dog. We conceded to Caroline's wisdom (she was brought up on a farm therefore the most likely to know) in guessing he was a Jack Russell terrier.

Once on the ground, his belly resting on the parquet floor of the porch, Winston remained in the same spot, hardly able to move with more than a feeble attempt at a strange waddle due to his extreme obesity. His short legs barely visible at each corner of his body, he panted with exhaustion, almost certainly causing considerable pressure on his heart.

"I need to give him his medication, nurse, if you don't mind, and then we'll go up and see the Major."

You didn't argue with Mrs Kilpatrick (Eleanor) who ran the house like a tight ship – or rather she commanded all the services who visited to do so. Her status had been elevated only slightly from housekeeper to wife when she finally married the Major with – according to the Major's only son, Robert, a university professor – barely a respectful gap between his own mother's death and their union. The word 'gold digger' was implied when I met Robert on one of his rare visits to his father.

The Major's first wife, (Robert's mother) Julia – almost thirty years his junior – was, according to Eleanor, 'a pretty and frail little thing.' Although she had financial means of her own, she had depended heavily on the Major emotionally and became jealous of his many trips abroad and, when at home, his almost nightly visits to his gentleman's club.

When Julia died – due to the permanent damage caused to her heart from a bout of rheumatic fever as a child – Eleanor wasted no time in stepping in to her shoes to 'comfort the poor Major.' We guessed Robert was in fear of losing his significant inheritance and that's probably why he put in the occasional appearance, although he was never able to hide his dislike for Eleanor, even though she continued to give his father care and attention following the massive stroke he had suffered only days after their wedding. We mused at our monthly team lunches if there might even have been a bit of 'rumpy pumpy' between the Major and Eleanor before Julia died.

In the kitchen, I watched as Winston greedily devoured the Milk Tray chocolate that concealed his 'heart' tablet, followed by the second sweet treat Mrs Kilpatrick gave him 'for being such a good boy' in swallowing the first. I decided not to give my thoughts about Winston's unhealthy eating habits as it was unlikely the damage could be reversed, surmising that they were probably the cause of his need for the medication in the first place. Instead, I edged towards the kitchen door eager to get started and attend to the Major.

Walking across the Minton-tiled hallway and up the

wide sweeping staircase reminded me of the mansion as I imagined it in the game of Cluedo, so I amused myself with dark thoughts of 'Professor Plum (Robert) murdering Mrs Peacock (Eleanor) with the candlestick in the library'. By the time I reached the top I was quite out of breath. Having walked to the end of the long landing I knocked politely on the door before entering the Major's bedroom.

I was greeted by the sight of a red-faced giant of a man sitting lopsidedly in the middle of hospital style adjustable bed, propped up by at least six fluffy pillows that seemed to be losing the battle of supporting his huge frame. As soon as he saw me in the doorway he began to emit a grunting sound, his face deepening to a beetroot colour. The stroke occurring in his left brain meant his speech was affected badly, leaving him with few comprehensible words and a paralysis on his right side. With his left hand, he pulled a large white handkerchief from beneath his right forearm which was fixed rigidly above his ample belly and useless for any other purpose aside from holding the handkerchief. He wiped the spit that had collected on his chin beneath his drooping right bottom lip.

Looking around the walls of the bedroom it was moving to see the many framed photos from the Major's earlier life. None of the usual family holiday snaps, smiling family groups or children posing for the school camera. All formal military shots: the Major sideways on, unsmiling, sporting his medals or inspecting his army proudly – sad reflections of a man who was now rendered almost helpless by his stroke.

Sally – the Major's other dog, a two-year-old Dalmatian – was languishing across the entire width of the foot of the bed, refusing to move before her belly had enjoyed a good rub from me. Finally satisfied she had received enough attention, she leapt from the bed and lolloped off into the corner, leaving behind a lengthy bloody streak – a reminder she was in season – on the otherwise crisp white top sheet. I ruminated the possibility that both dogs in the house were spoilt but with little time to ponder on how people's hygiene standards varied, I set about helping the Major get up to use the commode. This change of position also served to relieve the pressure on his bottom – an area particularly prone to skin breakdown when he had one of his frequent languishing-in-bed days spent gazing out of the window which overlooked the rolling lawn at the back of the house.

Watched suspiciously by Sally, I took the large ceramic rose-painted jug from the dresser, filled it with hot water from the sink in the corner of the room and poured it into the matching bowl. Using one of the two flannels, the pink for face and body, rubbing it over the tablet of red carbolic smelling Lifebuoy soap, I began the mission of bathing the Major's vast expanse of body. I had to refill the bowl several times as the water cooled and pay particular attention to his pressure areas – elbows, shoulder blades and heels – that might have been in danger of developing into sores as they were in constant contact with the bed due to his great weight and immobility.

The Major seemed to enjoy the pampering from the little grunts he made, and when almost every nook and cranny of flesh was washed, there was only one area left. Having been forewarned by Eleanor that, "The Major is more than capable of washing his own 'privates'", I had no intention of disagreeing with her and cringed as I remembered an embarrassing experience on the orthopaedic ward early on in my training.

I'd had been asked to help a patient wash and when I went behind the curtains that were drawn around his bed, found a man not much older than my eighteen years with both his arms encased in plaster of Paris at right angles to his body, rendering him helpless to do anything with the rapidly cooling plastic bowl of water that had been left for him to have a wash, presumably by another student either with a sense of humour or no common sense. Starting at the top, I tentatively worked my way down his (quite attractive) muscular body very slowly so as to delay attending to the inevitable area as long as possible, in the faint but unlikely hope that I'd be called away on an emergency before I reached it. Unable to delay any longer, I was just about to 'grab the bull by the horns', as it were, when the curtains opened and the patient's wife appeared. Before she could speak I pushed past her, slapping the sopping wet flannel into her hand and mumbling something about having an urgent task to attend to.

Trying to erase this painful memory, I vigorously applied soap to the blue flannel – put aside for the purpose – and placed it defiantly into the Major's 'good hand', looking away quickly and busying myself with removing the canine-soiled top sheet from the bed to avoid the Major's no doubt disappointed look.

Grateful for the assistance of the manual hoist, I rolled him from one side to the other to place the slings underneath him and then hooked them up to the metal arms of the hoist. Finally, I hand wound the mechanism which raised him above the bed. He swung in the air in an unseemly fashion for a minute until I lined the hoist up with the commode and wound the handle to lower him onto it. He giggled – his stroke often caused him to display inappropriate emotions – and huffed and puffed throughout the entire manoeuvre which, even with the help of the equipment, still involved a considerable effort.

I completed other tasks, which included emptying his catheter drainage bag, changing the bottom sheet, tidying around and replacing a small dressing on a leg wound which had developed from an infected flea bite, probably from one of the dogs. I chatted to him as I worked, about the news and my family. He joined in with various grunts, sounding surprisingly jolly considering his own restricted lifestyle. Repeating the transfer in reverse and making him comfortable in bed, I washed my hands and put on my coat to leave just as the Major dropped one of his tablets which promptly rolled under the bed. I bent down to retrieve it and suddenly felt a sharp slap on my bottom.

"MAJOR!"

It was at this moment that the bedroom door opened, and Mrs Kilpatrick walked in carrying Winston under her arm.

"GEOFFREY! Are you up to your tricks again? That's twice this week! I'm so sorry, nurse. You'll stop coming here if he carries on like this. He never used to be this rude. He really is so sorry."

I had my doubts about that and these were confirmed when, as I headed for the door, I glanced round at the Major who, seemingly quite unperturbed after his telling off, with his one good eye, gave me a cheeky wink.

Mr Lloyd?

- A STORY OF THE WRONG TROUSERS

There is something that feels quite empowering about wearing a uniform, particularly when it reassures patients and their relatives to have confidence in you. There are other times when you would like to pirouette in a swirl of smoke, like a Wonder Woman transformation in reverse, shedding the responsibility of your uniform forever.

It was interesting to note how patients, as soon as they walked onto a hospital ward, would tend to do as they were told without question. "Put on your pyjamas/get into bed/go to the toilet." (Even more powerful commands when delivered by the strict authoritarian matrons). This is possibly because as a patient feeling nervous about what we are about to face catapults us back in time to being vulnerable children. Or maybe it's to do with bargaining?

"If I do as I am told, God/ Doctor/Surgeon/ The Universe will make me get better quicker/ save me."

It was this blind trust of anyone in uniform that leads to my next story.

As the nights drew in, getting around from house to house became more difficult. Of course, there were our 'regulars', and even with my poor sense of direction, my car could have almost driven itself to them without any interference from me. Overall, we got to know the area very well, and anyway it was my home town so I was fairly confident driving around it. On a good night we could each comfortably visit eight or so local patients.

The outlying villages, however, were a different matter and I was not as familiar with navigating them. With their narrow winding roads, little if any street lighting and unpredictable house numbering, it would have been a challenge for anyone, let alone a dyslexic, inexperienced district nurse with poor night vision and an unreliable Hillman Imp that had a collection of unaffordable-to-fix-on-her-single-parent-income mechanical faults.

So when a new out-of-town patient appeared on the list it could be a bit of a lottery as to when the nurses would arrive. They were not easily beaten and determined not to let their patients down – so they always got there in the end.

Mr Lloyd was one of these lottery winners. The hospital had referred him for a one-off visit to give him an enema. For those of you who don't know about this procedure, it is a method where a bag of fluid – about 120 millilitres – is 'injected' into the rectum via a long tube, usually administered to clear out the contents of the bowel. In Mr Lloyd's case, this was needed to enable the radiographer to get a good look at his innards via X-ray the following day.

Yes, sounds horrible, doesn't it? I can tell you it is as I had personally experienced this undignified, embarrassing, and in my case, explosive procedure prior to giving birth to my youngest daughter. Enemas were then part of a regular childbirth routine – the reason given was that it might trigger labour, but I believe it was really to save the midwife the inconvenience of clearing up after what was already a messy business becoming an even messier one.

The small plastic-tubed bags that we carried with us were slightly lightly less messy and easier to administer than earlier nursing days when the dreaded enema liquid was poured from a jug into a funnel held high above the patient and via a long red rubber tube was delivered by gravity into the patient. However, it still was no less unpleasant.

The village seemed deserted. After having negotiated my way up and down the slender road off the main street several times, I was becoming more and more disorientated from peering out of the car window in the dark at the seemingly unfathomable system of house numbers which went from 6-21 on one side of the road and 2-18 on the other, with a 'Rose Cottage' and 'Cosy Nook' in the middle that had no numbers at all. Reaching the end of the street involved a risky seven-point turn – a dangerous manoeuvre but essential in order to avoid ending up in the beck that flowed there. This would be a catastrophe and too much for my poor little car that already bore many scars from previous encounters.

Having avoided by a whisker both a night shift farmer's tractor with no lights and a large chicken who was crossing the road (I don't know why), I eventually arrived at Mr Lloyd's tiny mid terraced cottage, relieved although more than a little flustered. Still, there was a job to be done, and unable to locate a door knocker or bell, I thrust my hand forward to bang on the rotting green painted door as hard as I dared, at the same time aware this might sound like a police raid to this sleepy village.

The door offered no resistance and losing my footing on the rain-sodden doormat, I was launched Superman-style straight into the living room, abruptly halting nose to nose with the cottage's inhabitant sitting in his armchair by a comforting open fire.

The middle-aged man – dressed in striped pyjamas, slippers and paisley dressing gown – didn't look at all surprised to see me, despite my dramatic entrance. Attributing this to the notion he was expecting my visit and that country folk are more relaxed than 'us townies', I took a small step back and feeling proud at the speed of my recovery enquired, "Mr Lloyd?"

Now on his feet, he was much taller than I imagined.

"Yes. What do you want?"

"Well let's go to your bedroom and then I'll explain more about the procedure."

Without protest, he led the way up the steep narrow stairway and directly into the only bedroom at the top. Looking around, I spotted a small white wicker chair peeking out from beneath a pile of clothes and manage to clear a space on it to lay my coat. There was no obvious resting place for my bag other than on the bottom of his bed and as he watched me open it and take out a pair of disposable gloves, his eyes widened in anticipatory anxiety.

"What do I do now?"

"Don't worry, this won't take long. If you could remove your pyjama bottoms and lie down on the bed on your left side…"

He complied without a word and I tucked a paper towel under his bottom and lifted his dressing gown, leaving just the relevant part of his anatomy visible for me to do my dirty work.

"Now if you could just bring your knees up a little…"

He obeyed, then without looking around, a decidedly wobbly voice came from the pillow where his head was buried: "Please can I ask why you are here?"

"Your X-ray? – Tomorrow? – Hospital? – Enema?"

My voice was growing weaker and fast losing ground with my final desperate plea, "Mr Lloyd?"

He got up from the bed a lot quicker than he had got on it.

"I don't think you want me."

Feeling quite sick and mumbling apologies, I gathered up my bag and coat under my arm and staggered down the stairs like a drunk on a Saturday night.

Would I be struck off the nursing register? Arrested for assaulting a patient? Too late, I remembered some good advice from my training days. 'Never say the patient's name, always ask, because most people when faced with someone in a uniform will assume you know best – even to the point of knowing their name better than they do.'

I could just hear him calling as I made my humiliating speedy exit.

"Mr Lloyd, you say? I reckon you want Harry at Rose Cottage – number 17. What's wrong with the silly old bugger now?" And chortling to himself, "Watch out when you're turning round at the beck."

The Saddest Work Of All

"I've learned that people will forget what you said, people will forget what you did, but people will never forget how you made them feel."

Maya Angelou.

Death brings out the best and the worst in families – sometimes denial, sometimes acceptance, and everything in between as patients and their loved ones negotiate the inevitable.

Although mostly the daytime district nurses were dedicated to their 'terminal' patients and often visited again in the evening to support them and their families, it was also a big part of the evening girls' role to visit, give pain and other symptom relieving medication and to settle them for the night.

Terminal care, or the much kinder term 'end of life care' or palliative care – used when a person has a life limiting illness, one that will more than likely be the cause of their death – was a very rewarding part of our work.

Contrary to popular belief – or is it hope? – it is very unusual for doctors to be able to predict with any accuracy when this death is likely to occur, although understandably the question is the most common one that people – once they have been given the diagnosis of such a condition – want to know the answer to. Some doctors, presumably feeling either helplessly unable to find a cure for their patient or wanting to appear all knowing and clever, may succumb under this pressure to come up with a response. The patient then either holds on to this as being true or, more often, in the slim hope of finding a more favourable answer, interrogates the next (in their eyes) professional lower down in the healthcare hierarchy for their verdict.

So, 'Not wanting to bother the doctor', this question often fell to the daytime district nurses to answer, and more often, in the dark of the evening when all looks bleaker and more frightening, to the evening girls. We took great care never to give our opinions about 'length of time', focusing instead on supporting the day nurses, Macmillan team, the Marie Curie night sitters and the patients' families to give our very best care and attention for however long it was required.

In any case, we had experienced on too many occasions for it to be a coincidence – with no scientific proof whatsoever aside from our own anecdotal testimonies – that often it is the patient themselves who takes charge of when they 'let go of life.'

Rose, a grandmother with a malignant brain tumour, 'given' three months by her doctor, who 'hung on' against all odds for a further year to attend her favourite grandson's wedding, only to pass away the following evening after the happy couple had gone on honeymoon.

Ninety-six year old Evelyn, a frail woman too weak to move and against all odds had survived without food or a drop of water passing her lips for three weeks. She shocked us one night when sitting bolt upright in bed, arms held out in front of her, announced to her long-deceased twin sister who she clearly could see in in the room, "I'm coming now." Sinking back into her pillows, she died minutes later.

So much we don't understand about life and death. Here are some more stories honouring the memory of others, all of them we supported to die where they wanted to remain – in their own homes.

Peter and Carol

- A STORY OF A LAST CHRISTMAS

Peter and Carol had led a comfortable life up until four years previously. Both had enjoyed satisfying careers – Carol a university lecturer and Peter a civil servant. Retiring at fifty-five and having no children, they were looking forward to having more time to spend with friends playing Bridge, gardening and holidaying abroad. Even with their busy individual working lives, they had never spent even one night apart.

It was at one of these Bridge evenings with their friends that Peter first noticed something was not well with Carol. Previously a competent player, she had started dealing the cards the wrong way and hadn't seemed to notice. There were other little signs too, like the time Carol had left the oven on after cooking dinner and when she had put the washing up liquid in the freezer.

Concerned, but unable to broach this with her, at first, Peter (on the advice of a friend) waited a few weeks before suggesting they go to see their GP. After some hospital tests it was confirmed that Carol had dementia. Peter and Carol were devastated – all their plans for a happy retirement dashed as Peter now becoming a reluctant but dedicated carer to his wife.

Carol's health declined rapidly and it was clear that Peter was struggling both physically and emotionally, even with the help of three visits a day from Home Helps and morning and evening visits from nurses.

Setting off to visit Peter and Carol, having enjoyed the best part of the day with my daughters, I was secretly pleased that they had been collected by their dad to spend the rest of the holiday with him as they were getting to the tetchy phase after all the excitement of opening their presents. Anyway, I loved working on Christmas Day, becoming used to it when I was training at the hospital, often volunteering to work having been then one of the nurses who didn't have children.

Ringing the bell at their spacious detached bungalow that had been adapted with a walk-in shower, grab rails and a track hoist to meet the ever- increasing physical deterioration of Carol, I thought it was unusual there was no answer. I remembered the patio doors at the back of the house were often open, and as it had been a mild December day – although the evening was getting a bit chilly now – I wondered if they may be enjoying some fresh air in their lovely garden that Peter had decorated with beautiful twinkling fairy lights to celebrate what might well be Carol's last Christmas.

When I walked around the side path I saw Carol sitting in her wheelchair on the patio shivering and crying quietly. I walked towards her, putting my arm around her shoulder.

"What's wrong, Carol? Where's Peter?"

Carol strained to hold her head up and as her eyes moved in the direction of the house, I spotted Peter through the open patio doors, lying on the floor. I rushed in, concerned about what I might find and kneeling beside him I tried frantically to remember the first aid training update I'd undertaken the previous year.

"Peter, Peter, can you hear me?"

It was clear he could not and had – by the colour and feel of his skin – been dead for several hours. There was sadly no need to recall any resuscitation procedure now. This was not the first time I'd come across an unexpected death but it was the first time I'd been on my own since my training without the reassurance of the hospital team behind me.

I used their telephone to call the ambulance. I guessed he may have had a heart attack, although I couldn't be sure so asked for the police as well and opened the front door ready for their arrival.

After wrapping a blanket around her shoulders, I pushed Carol in her wheelchair into the house. I was unsure if Carol realised what had happened or it may have been the shock. She seemed very confused.

"Put a blanket on him, nurse, he will be cold," she sobbed through her tears.

I did as she asked to comfort her and we sat in silence with Peter until the emergency services arrived and I explained the situation to them.

An hour later, when Peter's body and Carol had been transported off to hospital, on my way to my next visit I reflected on the evening so far. The sadness of a carer dying before his adored wife who was up to that point the sicker of the two. Maybe subconsciously he knew he had already lost her to the cruellest of illnesses and he couldn't cope with the thought of another Christmas without her. If only I had come a bit earlier – could I have saved him? What would happen to Carol now?

When I got home, I sat in the darkness of my living

room, pleased to spend some time alone and not having to feign any Christmas cheeriness for my children. I wondered what would happen to them if I should die suddenly. Dark thoughts and a stark reminder to make happy memories before memory is lost forever.

Mrs Taylor

- A STORY OF SELFLESSNESS

As I walked into the kitchen I was confronted by the three daughters of Mrs Taylor. One blocked my way to the staircase which led to Mrs Taylor's bedroom, the other two – slighter in build than their older sister but nonetheless menacing – stood one each side of me as if ready to eject me a bit like a nightclub bouncer might if I'd made a wrong move and tried to enter.

"Mum's doing a bit better today. The doctor said things are looking hopeful."

Although knowing they were hanging on to false hope and Mrs Taylor's liver cancer was reaching the end stage, I didn't see any point in replying, knowing from previous confrontations with this tight-knit family that any response held the danger of being misinterpreted. However, while not feeling able to disillusion them, I had no reservations about answering honestly if Mrs Taylor asked any questions about her condition.

Eventually when they were satisfied that I was suitably 'primed' to go upstairs, my path cleared, and heading for the bedroom I heard a final insistent, "Whatever you do, don't you dare tell mother how ill she is."

Walking into the tiny bedroom, it felt cold and bleak. Mrs Taylor was reluctant to put on the heating as she didn't want to spend the little money she had on her own comforts – rather saving it to go to her beloved daughters – their inheritance. Although I warmed to her because of her self-sacrifice, I couldn't help but feel angry at their thoughtlessness in allowing her to live in hardship more than she needed to.

Seeing Mrs Taylor's feeble and increasingly startlingly bright yellow body in the large divan bed, it was obvious she had deteriorated greatly in the couple of days since my last visit and probably didn't have long to live. I really liked this warm, friendly lady who was much more amenable than her daughters.

She greeted me in a low whisper. "Did you have a nice day off, nurse? I bet your children loved having you around."

Poignant words from this lovely lady who had enjoyed hearing the story of when we were at the seaside and the wind blew off my hat – my own two daughters screaming with laughter as we chased it all the way along the beach, and getting ice-creams as a reward when they finally retrieved it.

Mrs Taylor smiled and then reached out her hand, indicating for me to come closer. Taking her hand I sat at her side on the edge of the bed – a reassurance I was certain would not be allowed in hospital. I had been dismayed at times during my training to experience the last dregs of authoritarian regimented nursing care from the earlier days where it was often more important to the older Ward Sisters to ensure patients' beds were tidy than to spend time listening to their worries. I didn't care about that here, pleased to be able to share this intimate moment with her. I leaned in nearer to catch her whispered words.

"Nurse, I want you to promise me you won't tell them how sick I am."

The next evening when I was on duty, there was an answerphone message from Mrs Taylor's daughter to say she had died earlier that morning. She still sounded angry and although I wished I could have left the customary bereavement visit to someone else, reluctantly I drove back to the house to collect the nursing notes, unused dressings and some of the smaller equipment, knowing that mostly people don't want to have the medical reminders around them at that sad time.

Mrs Taylor's eldest daughter answered the door.

"Oh it's you again! Well I hope you're satisfied with what you've done. We warned you about telling Mum and now she's gone and it's all your fault! We fully intend to report you!"

I was shocked. Even knowing the angry words were probably spoken in grief, it was still upsetting to hear them. Even more shocking, when going up to the bedroom, Mrs Taylor's other two daughters and their husbands, along with another man I'd not seen before, were clearing the dressing table of all the jewellery that their Mum had treasured.

We saw this time after time. Families appearing like a plague of termites clearing a log pile – some even never having visited during their loved ones' illness but still there at the end taking their inheritance. As I left two of them arguing about a necklace, I couldn't help feeling happy that Mrs Taylor could not see what was happening in her family.

Emily

- A STORY OF DENIAL

Emily was a woman you might have described as vulnerable. Not that she was unintelligent or lacked capacity, just seemingly very shy, naïve and very apologetic – for everything. Her petite stature added to her childlike appearance although she was in her early forties. She was married to Alan, who she assured us was, "a lovely kind man" and we were surprised that we had never met her husband on our visits.

Emily had worked as a secretary at the doctor's surgery where she was also a patient. Her medical records were quite thin with very few entries– childhood mumps, a patch of eczema on her arm, common, insignificant illnesses, until recently.

She had tripped over a box of files that someone in the office had left by her desk, and holding her hand out to break her fall, landed badly on it, leaving her wrist looking quite red and swollen.

"It's nothing," she had insisted, never having been known to complain about anything.

It was a few days later when her colleagues eventually

convinced her to: "Let doctor have a look at it." Hesitantly, she 'popped in' to see the kindly Doctor Byrne, timidly knocking on his consulting room door apologetically, finding a space between his afternoon surgery patients.

He tried to take a closer look at her wrist but even in the sweltering heat of the August day she was wearing several layers of clothing which he had to encourage her gently to remove so he could examine her properly. She was only persuaded to do so in the presence of one of the practice nurses.

As layer after layer of a thick woollen cardigan, a baby pink jumper and a camisole top were unwillingly removed by Emily, a vile smell began to fill the room. Even the experienced nurse – unphased by most of the horrors she had witnessed in her long career – couldn't help but gag in the oppressive heat and the acrid smell emanating from Emily. Finally, it was revealed that the stench was coming from the watery blood-stained patch now exposed on the left cup of Emily's bra.

Doctor Byrne remained amazingly calm as he, in his melodic Irish accent gently asked, "How long have you had this, Emily?"

"Oh it's nothing, Doctor. It's getting better now; it's just a little scratch."

It was like walking onto a stage and adopting an actor's role when we visited Emily at home for her second visit of the day to change the dressing on the extensive fungating cancer that had rapidly devoured most of her left breast and was now gobbling greedily into her chest wall. Emily's house was spotless. Did she notice the awful smell generated by her wound or had she managed to somehow deny that too by spending hours each day scrubbing and cleaning?

Her endless babble throughout our visit left us little time for a response.

"I think it's starting to heal, don't you think, nurse?" was unnerving, although we felt obliged to play our part in the drama. Crushing her denial would have been cruel as it was the only way she could cope with the stark reality of her horrendous situation and the fear of the more than likely major haemorrhage that would end it.

As I soaked and gingerly removed the many layers of gauze padding, I felt like a bomb disposal expert, holding my breath not just to prevent the foul smell entering my nostrils but in case I might be the one unlucky enough to disturb a major blood vessel that was now so close to the surface.

As our relationship developed, Emily began to share more of her story, feeling able to trust us with things she had never been able to tell anyone. How she had never allowed her husband to see her undressed, how she had tolerated the shame of him "taking his marital rights", always in the dark. Most shocking was her story of the dead baby that she delivered in her lunch break, alone on her living room floor. Unaware she was pregnant until she had some stomach cramps, she singlehandedly wrapped the (at a guess from her description) four-month-old foetus in newspaper, put it in the kitchen bin and returned to work for the afternoon shift.

We were all equally relieved and saddened to hear of Emily's death, which was in the end thankfully quick and painless. The rupture of a major blood vessel had occurred suddenly during one of the day nurse's visits. Sadly, the nurse was powerless to stem the flow and within minutes – even before the ambulance had arrived – Emily was gone. Had she been in hospital – something she always refused –

there may have been an option to prolong her life for a little longer, but her life ended in the way she wanted, with no fuss.

Patricia

- A STORY OF FAITH

Although I have no religious beliefs, Patricia was my idea of someone who embodied Christian values – caring and compassionate towards others, never judgmental and a great listener. I felt better after a visit to Patricia. Always welcoming, she seemed to want little from me and I never left her home without feeling a warm, comforting glow.

Personal care is such an intimate act and she put me at ease while assisting her with hers in the evening. In her late fifties and having no children of her own, Patricia also seemed to enjoy my visits – or at least she never let on if she didn't – patiently and with interest listening to my problems with my children, my ex-husband and even the scary Mrs Hardy. My visits to her reminded me of the warmth my own mother had lacked.

It was not often we attended patient's funerals but when Patricia died quite suddenly from a condition quite unrelated to her cancer, I carried out the customary bereavement visit and asked her husband if he would mind me attending the service.

A week later, on a sunny Saturday morning, I dressed

respectfully in my uniform, arriving at the modern evangelical church for the 'Celebration of Patricia's life'. Finding a space at the back of the church where, although hoping I wouldn't be noticed, I stood out like a policeman at a rave – everyone else being dressed in brightly coloured clothes.

Despite the completely different setting, I couldn't help but recall my own mother's funeral a few years earlier – a very different and formal catholic ceremony when the priest at the graveside paused from his religious ramblings to chastise me for crying, telling me I should be happy that my mother was now free from suffering and had gone to a better place.

I tried to join in with all the happy clapping but when the minister leading the service spoke about Patricia's life and how anyone who visited her received much more than they gave, it was too much for me and my tears flowed. I was immediately surrounded by some of Patricia's friends from the church throwing their arms around me and telling me not to be sad but to be happy for Patricia.

I didn't feel happy at that moment and didn't want to intrude further in their seeming jolly service, so making my excuses at the first opportunity, I left quietly reflecting on my way home whether nurses were allowed to have feelings or at least openly show them and how differently people find ways to express their grief.

Steve's Mum

- A STORY OF PROFESSIONAL RESPONSIBILITY

Predictably, in a town the size of ours, the nurses would occasionally come across people they knew in a different context, who had then become our patients. Even so, I was still a little taken aback when Steve answered the door of the newly referred terminally ill patient who I realised was his mother.

I remembered Steve well from my junior school. He was always in trouble, a real bad boy, although he had that cheeky charm that always managed to ensure he didn't get caught, at least not for anything too serious.

When we got older and went to different secondary schools, I didn't see him again until my late teens. When out and about with friends in the town pubs I would often bump into him out with his gang – usually on a Friday night and, more often than not, he would be involved in or likely the instigator of some sort of altercation. Although by then a heavy drinker, he still managed to keep his roguish smile and keep out of prison – unlike his father who had been in and out of there for most of Steve's childhood and early adult life. It was hard not to have a soft spot for Steve even though he had broken the hearts of more than a couple of my friends over the years.

Now it was his eyes that were red and clearly not just from an excess of alcohol but from crying. I was sure he recognised me as there were a few seconds of awkwardness before he said, "Come in, nurse, but you're too late. Mum's just gone," before throwing his arms around me in a bear hug that took my breath away and bawling loudly.

When he finally pulled back, looking ruefully down at his feet but still with the cheeky smile I remembered so well, he regained some level of control with, "So, I'm almost an orphan now. We're just waiting for the doctor to come. Would you like to see her?"

Still recovering from the unexpected hug and never having met Steve's mum, I didn't want to stay but it felt somehow wrong to leave him alone. Hearing myself say, "Of course, I'd love to…", I followed Steve into the front room which had been converted into a makeshift bedroom to nurse his mum in the final stages of her illness which had come unexpectedly suddenly, hence the late call on our services.

She looked very peaceful, almost asleep – her shoulder length dark hair was unkempt and strands stuck to the side of her face on one side which was still clammy with perspiration.

"Would you like me to tidy her hair and freshen her up a little?"

"That would be lovely, nurse – a woman's touch."

He watched helplessly, childlike as I reached into the bedside cupboard for a hairbrush and a sponge. In silence I filled a bowl with warm water from the sink in the kitchen and gently sponged his mum's face and hands and carefully brushed, her hair, arranging it on the pillow.

Smoothing the duvet and spraying it with a little

perfume, I placed Mrs Williams's arms by her side, not knowing how long it would be before the doctor's and then the undertaker's visit. (We were taught to do this for very practical reasons as a body can stiffen up quickly after death). Taking a single white rose from an arrangement in a vase by the bed and laying it on the pillow, I took a step back to stand beside Steve, feeling content with my work.

Through his tears and using my name now: "Thank you, Alice, she looks beautiful."

I would have happily left then, giving Steve some private time reflecting on how peculiar our work was, in that it was possible to have such a personal and rewarding experience in the middle of a busy evening with a complete – and indeed dead – stranger. However, there was still one task left to do.

In the early 1970s, syringe drivers – a way of given a measured dose of medication evenly over a twenty-four-hour period – were only just coming into use. So, for most patients, the only option available to those who needed more intensive pain relief or who were no longer able to swallow oral medication, was to give an ampoule of (usually) diamorphine – a controlled drug via an intra muscular injection – sometimes up to every four hours. I was always very cautious when having to administer any medication, checking and double checking all the details probably more obsessively than the rest of the team, due to a bad experience early in my nurse training – a potentially more serious error than the mix up with Mr Lloyd.

It was my first week on the busy men's surgical ward. Up until then I'd only been working under strict guidance in the hospital departments and wards as a cadet. The busy Staff Nurse handed me a small medicine pot containing two strong pain relief tablets and told me to give them to a patient who was recovering from a major surgical procedure.

The correct process was that a trainee nurse would be accompanied by someone more senior to check the patient's name on their wristband and stay until the medication was swallowed, given that anything could happen between it leaving the pot and reaching the patient's stomach.

Seeing she was busy and a bit huffy, without questioning the Staff Nurse, I did as I was told, thus in my mind saving her the trouble and hopefully gaining some brownie points on my first ward. I was pleased to have remembered the protocol, staying by the patient's bed until the moment he had consumed the tablets – even asking if he wanted more water to make sure he had swallowed them. The next part came in horrifyingly slow motion as it dawned on me that this was not the patient who had had the major surgery but a minor procedure for which strong pain relief was not required.

I ran into the sluice, staring aimlessly at the racks of gleaming stainless bedpans, and there followed an agonising few minutes that seemed like hours. What had I done? What if I'd killed him? Peeping out of the door and down the long Nightingale-style ward, seeing the 'poisoned' patient was still sitting up in bed and looking quite well, I toyed with the idea of not telling anyone, but even in my confused mind I knew, in reality, it was not an option to stay quiet.

First I confessed to the Staff Nurse who, to be fair, knew she bore some responsibility for the error. Rapidly the awful news shot up the ranks to the Ward Sister – an intimidatingly efficient Scot – and within five minutes all hell was let loose. Everyone seemed to be looking at me as I

– feeling like a murderer by now – tried to carry on with my duties with shaking hands.

Two Senior Nursing Officers (these had recently replaced matrons but were none less scary) appeared from nowhere and an urgent meeting was set up in Sister's office to decide my – and assess the patient's – fate.

When finally summoned by Sister MacKintosh, it had been agreed that no real harm had been done and no further action would be taken, apart from my being required to receive additional training around medication administration.

The patient was never told of the error – an inconceivable prospect these days where I'm sure a huge enquiry would be launched.

Although on a late shift the next day, after a sleepless night I went in early to check that my victim was still alive. To my relief he was dressed and sitting by the side of his bed ready to go home. He looked very pleased, if not a little high.

"I'm feeling fantastic, nurse! I don't know what those pills were you gave me but I had the best night's sleep I've ever had. Didn't feel a thing after my op. I was wondering if you might be able to get me some more to take home."

As Mrs Williams had died at home and had been prescribed diamorphine injections, the remaining ampoules had to be accounted for. This would be done on the ward or in the pharmacy in the case of a hospital death. As District nurses, we weren't allowed to transport controlled drugs in our cars. The safest option was to check, count and record the surplus and then – witnessed by a relative – destroy them in the patient's home. Explaining this to Steve, I asked him to agree the number of ampoules as I counted them in front of him, placing them on a paper towel which I then folded over.

"Do you have a rolling pin please?" (The usual implement people offered to crush the glass ampoules).

Steve disappeared for a moment, and rummaging around in the cupboard under the stairs, popped his head out.

"Will this do, nurse?"

As I methodically completed the destruction with the empty beer bottle, I wondered what Mrs Hardy might say.

I never saw Steve again but heard a few years later that sadly his alcohol addiction had finally got the better of him and he had died from liver disease.

Julia

- A STORY OF THE DESTRUCTION OF A FAMILY

Inevitably, all the deaths we encountered were sad. Many of our end of life care patients were in their sixties and beyond, but when we visited a much younger person, the loss brought an extra layer of heartache, both for their families and for us.

Julia was in her late twenties – not much older than me – with two children, boys aged five and seven, a beautiful modern home and a loving husband. She would have had a perfect life had it not been for the cruel Motor Neurone Disease (MND) that had weakened the muscles in her legs and arms, leaving her having to use a wheelchair and needing help with all personal care.

There wasn't and still isn't a cure for MND and we all knew that the way Julia's disease was progressing – more than likely next affecting the muscles she needed to swallow and finally to breathe – left a very frightening prospect as her death approached.

Our visits were often chaotic when Julia's children were there. Julia's husband, Richard, had immersed himself in his work and was usually absent. Julia's worsening condition, leading to her increasing helplessness to be a 'normal' mother to her children, was very upsetting for us to witness — especially those of us with our own children. As a single mum, I couldn't contemplate what would happen if I had an illness like that. How would I cope?

It was inconceivable to imagine fully what it was like for Julia to experience not only the physical impact of this dreadful disease, but also the emotional sense of loss as her body rapidly and systematically failed her.

Julia's children — as children do — took advantage of their mum's inability to discipline them from her wheelchair and they would often take money from her purse or do other little acts of naughtiness with Julia powerless to stop them.

Julia, having lost her own mother at a young age, relied on her husband's mother, Eileen, to help her with much of her daily care and care of the children. Eileen did this with more than a fair amount of resentment. She was a very outspoken woman who had no issue with telling us and anyone else who visited — even in front of the children — how devastated she felt that her son had ended up with such a 'damaged' woman. We all found this abhorrent. However, it was important we kept the peace as everyone, including Eileen's husband — an inoffensive man quite the opposite of his wife — was afraid of Eileen 'exploding' in case she walked out for good. Julia depended on her input and was forced to tolerate her vicious tongue. Julia's husband also seemed to walk on eggshells around his mother — fearful of challenging her verbal attacks on his wife.

Julia was deteriorating rapidly. It seemed every time I visited she had lost a little more of her ability to function — her facial muscles had weakened further and breathing was becoming an effort, as was my learning to interpret her slurred speech. First checking Eileen was well out of earshot, we would share whispered silly mother-in-law jokes.

"Where's the wicked witch of the west today?" would make Julia giggle hoarsely – a lighter moment of relief from her suppressed anger and fear.

We also shared tears – both knowing, without the need for words, that there wasn't much time left.

When I arrived that evening, the house was almost in darkness apart from the porch light and there was no need for any explanation as Julia's husband opened the front door with his coat on and a small bulging carrier bag in his hand.

Making no eye contact with me, he said, "Everything's been arranged. I'm just going to stay at Mum's. The boys are already there. I'm so sorry."

He pushed past me to get into his car. I stood for a moment before getting into my own car, numb at the coldness of his departure. I switched on the radio, needing distraction before moving on to my next visit.

'Ain't no sunshine when she's gone. It's not warm when she's away…'

I managed to somehow drive to the next street before pulling over and sobbing. Julia's last days had been made all the more painful by the anger of her mother-in law. It just seemed so cruel that she wasn't allowed to enjoy them freely with her children and husband.

The Dark Side Of Caring

"Resentment is like taking poison and waiting for the other person to die."

Carrie Fisher

Most families muddle through reasonably well when a family member has a short-term illness. However, when that illness becomes prolonged, or even permanent and disabling, there are more serious challenges as family dynamics change and wives/ husbands/ children are required to become – sometimes reluctantly – carers. We witnessed already difficult relationships become compounded when people took on these caring responsibilities, raising old resentments and bringing new ones.

People are resilient and they find ways to cope, sometimes by dissociating. Like Julia's husband, Richard, who spent most of his time at work in an attempt to distance himself from the pain of imminently losing his wife or indeed cope with his mother's anger. People manage as best they can. Who are we to judge? Over time, we encountered the reality of how caring took its toll emotionally and often walked into some quite disturbing situations which had all but broken down.

Mr Lyttle

- A STORY OF GUILT

Fitting for his name, Tom Lyttle was a short, scrawny, angry red-faced man. His wife, Gwen, was the opposite both in build and temperament – at least on the outside.

She had taken to their double bed ten years previously following a stroke and filled it with her huge obese form, which seemed to expand by the week, leaving no room for her husband. Everyone assumed at first this was what caused much of the tension in their relationship.

He took his anger out on everyone, including us nurses.

"You're late!" "You're early!" "The doctor hasn't been yet. Are you sure you asked him?"

We could do nothing right as he raged, his veins throbbing in his temples. Even when I was late one night because of an emergency call, he showed no understanding.

"You think everyone else is more important than my wife!"

Gwen just lay like a queen ruling over her kingdom and watching her husband's outbursts with a smug smile.

She could have sat out in her chair or even gone out in the wheelchair – adapted to accommodate her large frame – but it stayed redundant in the understairs cupboard since her stroke with her flatly refusing to use it, saying she preferred her husband's company. So he remained a virtual prisoner attending to her every need. If he wanted to go out – even to the corner shop – she would make such a fuss that he very rarely went beyond their back garden.

The only exception was on a Friday evening when at seven o'clock Gwen would give him fifty pence from the purse she kept under her pillow. He would put on his thirty-year old navy suit, Brylcreem the few remaining strands of black hair to his shiny scalp and trot half a mile down the hill to The Feathers pub. There he would down a half pint of bitter, followed by a tot of dark rum walking back up the hill to be home for quarter to eight.

It was discovered when talking to a receptionist at the doctor's surgery (whose husband also drank at The Feathers) that this was the pub where – around ten years ago just previous to her stroke – Gwen had taken a little stroll down to meet Tom and found him 'in the arms of another woman.' It seemed he had been paying for his dalliance ever since.

Aside from the pub on a Friday evening, his garden was the only place where he relaxed, growing amazingly healthy-looking vegetables and flowers. His runner beans could have won awards in a show if only he had been 'allowed out' to attend one. If we could calm him enough to get him outdoors to his beloved refuge in the lighter evenings after we had attended to his wife, he was transformed from Hyde to Jekyll. Chatting proudly about his latest horticultural achievement – dividing his Dahlias, planting his peas, sowing his salvias – he was a changed man, even on occasions giving us brown paper bags generously full of his homegrown tomatoes and runner beans.

The remainder of his time was – on Gwen's insistence – spent carrying out most of her personal care. Adding to his frustration of lack of intimacy with his wife, he washed, dried and creamed every fold and crease of her ample body while she lay motionless, even though she had recovered much of her mobility shortly after her stroke. Although it was obvious Tom was bitter about his lot in life, he did his job very efficiently, taking great care of his wife's pressure areas, particularly the vast expanse of buttocks – which although completely flat from the years of contact with the mattress, had never shown any sign of skin breakdown.

The reason for my visit, as it almost always was, was to find out why Gwen's catheter – the tube that went into her bladder and was attached to a drainage bag hung on the bottom of the bed frame – wasn't draining properly. This had become a weekly occurrence – strangely, late on a Friday night.

One of the common problems preventing catheters from draining properly was a bladder infection that caused the tube to become clogged up. This was usually because the patient didn't drink enough fluids to keep the tube flushed out and clear from all the bacterial gunk that had accumulated in it.

Tom seemed a little more jovial and even more red faced than usual. Maybe it was the fact that he'd been set free for an hour at the pub or maybe he'd sneaked an extra tot of rum? I took a flannel and the strong-smelling Palmolive soap that Gwen loved. I washed and dried the area, taking care to clean carefully around the outer tube of the catheter where it entered her body. However, as I got closer to investigating the obstruction to Gwen's catheter, it became apparent that going to the pub wasn't the only little pleasure Gwen allowed Tom on a Friday night!

Michael

- A STORY OF RECIPROCAL ABUSE

Michael was in his early forties and unfortunate enough to
have a progressive type of Multiple Sclerosis (MS). He
lived in what was judgementally – but probably accurately
– known as 'the rough area of town' where the (mainly)
council houses were run down and uncared for, as were
many of the residents and their children. Michael, his wife
Sonia, his six children – ranging from 12 to 3 years old –
along with their aggressive unruly Alsatian dog, lived in
one of most decrepit.

The informally named 'tin houses' – actually made of
steel – had been erected after the war as a temporary
housing measure and should by rights have been
demolished twenty years previously as they were found to
be a fire risk, but councils devoid of money and desperate
to house 'problem' families such as Michael's jumped at
the chance to maintain these ghetto-like estates. Except
they didn't really maintain them to any decent standard,
leaving the already disadvantaged residents even more
demoralised.

More often than not, our visits to Michael were to try

to manage his catheter – which like Mrs Lyttle's, regularly became blocked. This blockage can lead to a medical emergency if left for more than a few hours, causing kidney damage if the urine can't escape. Unlike Mrs Lyttle, however, the blockage in Michael's case was not usually due to an infection but caused by an external constriction.

Michael's MS had gradually weakened him, leading him to have many falls due to his unsteady gait to use a manual wheelchair. Being unable to manoeuvre it very easily on his own, he relied mostly on his wife but often his children to push him around. Many a car would be heard screeching to a halt to avoid hitting them on one of their crocodile route marches to the park when the dog, completely out of control, pulled wildly on the lead that was attached to the wheelchair handles. Or the children could be found taking turns to push each other in Michael's wheelchair, playing 'chicken' across the busy road, leaving him at home stranded in bed and powerless to stop them.

We found the visits to Michael's home hectic and frustrating, and it was the third time that week we'd been called in to "bloody come and sort him out" as Sonia had angrily put it in her request left on the answering machine at the nursing base. This time it was my turn to visit.

I drew up at the familiar front door – shamefully identifiable as 'council' by the dark green paint that was applied to all the houses in the estate, this one having the additional deep slashes from the family dog's claws making it look like some wild animal had attempted to break in.

After hammering on the door for several minutes the loud music that blared out was eventually silenced and replaced with Michael's voice shouting, "SHANNON! Open the door for the nurse!" The snotty nosed three-year-old opened the door wearing only a towelling nappy which was barely held in place by a giant safety pin. Sonia had – according to Michael – "gone to the bingo; she was fed up of waiting for you".

I was concerned about the young children being left in the care of their father, who could barely look after himself, but also quite pleased that she wasn't there as she constantly shouted at Michael, handled him very roughly and goaded the children to do the same.

It didn't take much investigation to see what was causing the catheter blockage. The bag was detached from its metal holding frame and the long tube wrapped tightly around the wheel of Michael's chair, causing it to kink and stop the flow of urine into the bag. It was hard to believe that Sonia hadn't noticed this before she went out as it was something she could have untangled quite easily herself. I even wondered if she had left it on purpose as she was constantly angry with Michael, seemingly seeking revenge for an unhappy marriage that bore his long history of infidelities, domestic abuse and failure to hold down a job prior to his MS. In her words, blaming him entirely for "making us end up in this shitty place."

I opened my nursing bag, having nowhere free to place it but on the very worn and decidedly grubby sticky carpet. Taking out some disposable gloves, I made a mental note to again contact the constantly exhausted social worker who was involved with the family, not wanting to write too much of my concerns in the nursing notes that remained in the patients' house for fear of Sonia reading them and possibly further taking her anger out on Michael or the children. I carefully untangled the tube and removed it along with the catheter bag, putting on my sterile gloves before replacing it quickly with a new one. Michael gave a sigh of relief as the urine flowed freely into the bag, almost filling it in one go.

"Dad's wet himself! Dad needs a nappy!" Shannon (the three-year-old) sang, poking him in his arm and dancing around him.

He could have been provided with a drainage bag with a shorter tube that would be hidden beneath his trouser leg, which would have been much more dignified, but we doubted if Sonia would 'remember' to empty that at all as it would be out of sight and this would pose more of a risk. I felt for him. Now he was the vulnerable one in the family and the children were encouraged by their mum to take out her anger on him.

Going to the kitchen to wash my hands, I searched without success for the clinical waste bag to dispose of the used catheter bag, finally finding it under the kitchen sink being used to store potatoes. Returning to the sitting room, I just managed to scoop up my bag from the floor before Shannon – clearly over excited from her dancing – vomited into it.

Mrs Hall

- A STORY OF PROTECTION

Mrs Hall was a gentle unassuming woman who – because of her disabling and painful arthritis – remained in her specially adapted armchair during the day. Her husband, Jim, was a man who hid his resentment well – or so he thought – caring for his wife's every need with a fixed smile that didn't fool us and made me feel a little uneasy when I visited to help settle Mrs Hall for the night. Mrs Hall never grumbled about her painful life and was always full of praise for her husband on whom she was totally dependent on for almost everything.

We had noted there was a bruise here, a red mark there, even when she had a broken arm – almost certainly all caused by Jim's careless handling of her at best, or at worst... well I didn't want to think about that. She never complained, saying, "He is a kind man" and "He doesn't mean it; he's just a bit clumsy."

There was a friend, Karen, a neighbour who was waiting on her own doorstep most evenings when we visited. She would bound over to me.

"Nurse, you must do something. You can see what he's

79

doing to her." Then she would walk into Mrs Hall's house behind me, saying with a half-smile, "He can't stop me visiting when you're there. He won't say anything rude to me in front of you."

And he didn't.

His smile just became more tense and he slunk off into the kitchen while Mrs Hall chatted with me and her neighbour, her gnarled hands held tight against her chest and her deformed contracted legs almost meeting them. In any of our chats, despite much probing and cajoling from Karen, Mrs Hall still refused to say a bad word against her husband so we felt powerless to do anything to protect her.

One night as I approached the house, Karen was standing in her doorway as usual, this time excitedly with her coat half on half off.

"I'm so glad you're here, nurse," she said, struggling to get her arm into the other sleeve of her coat. "I have a little present for Gladys."

She went back into her house for a moment then returned, almost pushing me over the doorstep into Mrs Hall's house.

Mr Hall, still smiling though unable to suppress a tut, disappeared as usual into the kitchen, clearly outnumbered by us women. Then out of the deep pocket of her raincoat, Karen produced a tiny Chihuahua dog, not much bigger than the palm of her rather large manly hand, with the biggest, most appealing innocent eyes.

Winking at me she said to Mrs Hall, "Gladys, this is Harry. I've brought him for you to look after."

Harry immediately snuggled down in Mrs Hall's lap and the three of us cooed and aahed over him – it was clear he had settled in to his new home. Mrs Hall looked delighted with her new baby, although she protested a little.

"How can I look after him when I'm stuck in this chair?"

Karen, determined Harry was going to stay, replied, "Don't you worry, Gladys. He doesn't take much looking after. I'll be able to check on him daily, feed him and take him for a little walk and to any vet's appointments. He's so needing a loving home."

She didn't need to say more it was clear from Mrs Hall's face as Harry snored gently in her lap that it was a done deal.

After a while, Mr Hall appeared in the kitchen doorway. Even though he hadn't spoken, Harry woke up with a start and began to emit a low growl which sounded surprisingly intimidating from such a tiny dog. The growl turned into a high-pitched bark and Harry leapt onto the floor from his snuggly resting place, yapping and yelping around Mr Hall's ankles before finally sinking his teeth into his trouser leg and hanging on while his victim leapt around the living room in a sort of maniacal dance for quite a few minutes until finally managing to shake his attacker off.

When she had stopped laughing, Mrs Hall calmly and in a very quiet voice called, "Harry", who without a yelp of protest, jumped back onto her lap, and clearly satisfied with his work, promptly went back to sleep.

We looked at each other and Karen, being the more forward, said in a voice loud enough for Mr Hall (who had returned to the kitchen in a huff) to hear, "Well, Gladys, it looks like you've got a little bodyguard now. You won't need to worry about anyone bothering you with Harry around."

Mum

- A STORY OF DEPENDENCE

There were many other incidents of encounters with children and animals but none so unusual as when we visited a woman to give her a pain-relieving injection as she was experiencing severe back pain.

It was another chaotic household much like Michael's, with several children running around and in the middle of the commotion was Mum, lying on the floor of the living room, rolling around and screaming in pain.

We suspected she may have become dependent on the prescribed diamorphine. This strength of drug was not usually given for a condition such as this, especially as there was no clear confirmed diagnosis. So even though we suspected it wasn't right, it was a brave nurse who questioned a GP's orders. It would have been futile in any case – her doctor being a Welshman with a bit of a temper, who readily prescribed pain relief as a first option, especially when eager to get away to watch his beloved rugby. We imagined she had probably made so much fuss on his home visit he had opted for the path of least resistance and prescribed what she wanted.

Not taking any chances, I prepared a space to draw up the injection as safely as I could, away from the children's reach. Almost before the needle had touched her buttock she lay back, sighing happily in instant delirious relief.

To add to the surreal drama of the situation, I was being carefully observed from the corner of the room by the beautiful brown eyes of the tiny Shetland pony that lived in the house.

Betrayal In Plain Sight

"The saddest thing about betrayal is that it never comes from your enemies, it comes from those you trust the most."

Anon

We often talked about our suspicions of carers having affairs. It was understandable that relationships of patients and their partners/ spouses were constantly under strain. Normally speaking of these infidelities were avoided on our visits but sometimes betrayals were in plain sight, saddening and angering us, leaving us with an uncomfortable feeling and wanting to protect our already unfortunate patients.

In addition, some of us, including myself, had experienced betrayal first hand so we were always going to be biased – if only in thought – towards our female patients.

Mrs Finlay

- A STORY OF SUFFERING IN SILENCE

When we first visited Mrs Finlay – a quietly spoken Scottish lady – in her small, terraced house, it was apparent she had already had more than her fair share of suffering.

Walking with difficulty due to having contracted polio as a child – her muscle-wasted legs were weak already – she had then been diagnosed with MS, making her even more frail. As if that wasn't enough, during the past few weeks she had also been having radiotherapy treatment for breast cancer, leaving her with some painful burns and blisters which required twice daily dressings. Even with all these problems, we were inspired at how independent she was. Often she had already struggled to get herself into bed when we arrived, not wanting to give us extra work to do.

Her husband, Don, went out every evening to the pub, too fixated on his night out to help his wife before he went. His only contribution was to deposit the front door key under the mat for us to let ourselves in to the small hallway leading to the living room where Mrs Finlay slept. Even that small task often eluded him, and I had to walk down to the pub on more than one occasion because he had forgotten to leave the key in his hurry to get away.

He didn't look too pleased at having his evening interrupted when I walked up to the bar where he was standing with some friends. I probably didn't hide my annoyance very well either, as it didn't endear him to me any more as he didn't even apologise.

Most times he wasn't home before we had left the house, which according to Mrs Finlay was after the pub closed. However, this evening she was being as stoically brave as always – even though I'm sure it must have been painful as I finished fixing the dressing to the burned area under her arm. We heard the front door click open and two voices, one obviously Don's and the other a woman, giggling and stumbling as they made no secret of the fact they were going upstairs.

In this awkward moment, there didn't seem to be anything to say. I remained silent to give Mrs Finlay the space to talk if she wanted to, not looking at her while I busied myself by tidying away the soiled dressings and putting on my coat.

Mrs Finlay said nothing.

As I was leaving, I offered, "I hope you're ok?"

"I'm fine, nurse. Could you put the radio on, please. It drowns out the noise from the street and helps me sleep."

Mrs Shaw

- A STORY OF THE PAINFUL TRUTH

Mrs Shaw had a degenerative inherited condition known as Huntington's Disease. It seemed once she had received her confirmed diagnosis at the age of fifty she appeared to decline very rapidly, and she was already experiencing the violent jerky movements more common in the later stages of the illness.

It was almost like she had given up when the fears she had lived with most of her adult life were realised. Having watched her mother suffer a horrible death – even though at the time the illness was not named – she had always known she was destined to meet the same end.

Unlike Mrs Finlay, she'd had no reservations about loudly telling her many visitors – both friends and family – that her husband was having an affair.

Mr Shaw was very attentive to his wife. In fact, a very sociable, likeable man generally – at least that's how we experienced him when we visited; admirable considering the strain he must have been under with his wife's illness.

Looking at the many wedding photos placed strategically around the bungalow's spacious modern living room, they portrayed a vibrant couple with so many hopes and dreams, it was hard to fathom how not so many years later their relationship could be reduced to almost a parent/ child one.

Like the shame experienced when your child has a tantrum in a supermarket, he would try to hide his embarrassment at his wife's accusations, denying them and trying to calm things by whisking her visitors swiftly away to the kitchen and making them tea where they could be heard talking in hushed voices.

He was so apologetic for her eruptions, talking only of his concerns for her, explaining that her thoughts were becoming distorted due to her worsening dementia – another outcome of the Huntington's. This did nothing to lessen the impact of her outbursts, however, during which she became very animated, making it even more distressing for all who witnessed them.

One evening it was unusually quiet in the house. There were no visitors and Mr Shaw let me in, his usual over-cheery self.

Aware Mrs Shaw's speech was becoming weaker and now barely distinguishable, I had to listen very carefully to understand what she wanted and to try my best to meet her needs. Her distress and anger that was once directed verbally at her husband was now mostly limited to erratic bodily movements – which somehow were even more unsettling to watch than hearing her slurred, anguished speech. Keeping my head low and close to her face to capture any hint of Mrs Shaw's whispers, I helped her to wash at the low sink in her specially adapted bathroom. There was a knock at the back door, and she suddenly became very disturbed, her flailing arm knocking my specs from my face.

I had met the neighbour who breezed into the

bathroom with a chirpy, "What's wrong, Audrey?" several times. She always seemed ready to help and had offered to collect prescriptions, do some shopping and even to take Mrs Shaw out in her wheelchair.

Her cheerfulness soon faded, and she looked uneasy at Mrs Shaw's response. Mrs Shaw had defiantly turned her head away from her neighbour, who looked relieved as Mr Shaw came in and, as always, awkwardly ushered the neighbour into the kitchen away from the disturbance – strangely, with no apologies to me this time.

I rescued my specs from the floor and as Mrs Finlay calmed a little, I resumed where I'd left off and began to smooth her shoulder length blonde hair that had become quite ruffled in her outburst.

There was no mistaking the words she uttered with more clarity and volume than I'd heard for a long time, and I knew then without a doubt our suspicions were correct.

"THAT'S HER!"

Team Spirit

- WHATEVER THE WEATHER, WORKING TOGETHER

"There's nothing like nursing friendships – you can discuss vomit and bowel movements at the lunch table and no one flinches."

Anon

I truly appreciated the welcome I received from the Evening Girls when joining the team and our relationships continued to cement and grow as we worked together.

Initially we worked our rounds alone but there were increasing concerns around safety – especially in badly lit and less salubrious areas of town and particularly during bad weather and when visiting patients in what came to be known as 'the rural.'

The snow had been particularly heavy that week in January. I hoped it might have cleared by the time I was due to start my shift at 6.30 p.m. but instead it seemed to be worsening, leaving me quite worried I set off in the eerie darkness.

The few cars I saw – and there weren't as many as usual at that time of night – all seemed to be travelling away from town, their drivers eager to get home before the top snow froze, making it even more treacherous. Or more likely after hearing the weather forecast, most people had left work early and were already enjoying their evening meal by the fire.

Shuddering with cold and wondering how (or even if) I was going to get around, I'd already telephoned from home those patients who had families who could assist them to ask if they would mind trying to manage without my help for the night.

Calling my colleague Caroline, who lived the other side of town, we agreed to divide the remaining patients between us. Feeling I had drawn the short straw with Miss Johnson, I resigned myself to the fact that I was out and about anyway so it wouldn't make much difference who I visited.

Mr Tyler

- A STORY OF LOST MEMORIES

My first call was to Mr Tyler, an eighty-year-old man who lived alone and was starting to become quite forgetful and deaf. He needed an evening insulin injection to ensure his blood glucose levels didn't get too high after eating his supper. His failing memory meant he could not always remember to do his finger prick test before administering his insulin – or on occasions he had been known to forget the insulin altogether.

I enjoyed my visits to him and although the purpose of the visit took only minutes, I often stayed to talk if I had some time, perhaps because he reminded me of my own father who sadly had died when my eldest daughter was nine months old. He had enjoyed a similar career to Mr Tyler in electronics. It was a mutually enjoyable visit as Mr Tyler had no family and loved hearing about mine.

As usual, when I knocked on the front door there was no reply, so I removed my glove and forcing my hand through the icy cold metal letterbox, I fumbled around, eventually locating the key that thankfully was hanging from a string on the other side.

The vast Victorian three storey house was in total darkness. Armed with my torch, I walked nervously along the hall in an effort to locate my patient. There was no response to my calling his name but then I heard a rustling noise that seemed to be coming from the understairs cupboard. More grunts and thumps ensued followed by a sharp "DAMMIT".

"Are you alright, Mr Tyler?" I shouted just as his (still amazingly full for his age) head of curly hair – more dishevelled than usual – emerged from the cupboard, followed by the rest of him holding a handful of randomly coloured wires in one hand and a flickering, dying torch in the other, looking like some sort of mad professor:

"I was just in the middle of rewiring the house and the lights went out," he said mournfully.

Not knowing where to start as there was so much wrong with this statement, I offered a practical suggestion.

"Do you think we could get the lights back on for a minute – maybe check the fuse box?" I asked hopefully.

"Oh you are a clever girl. You must take after your dad," he replied, ducking down and disappearing into the cupboard again.

Hoping my suggestion wouldn't make things worse and put him at further risk, I stood with my fingers tightly crossed. Thankfully, after what seemed like an age, the lights came on and a muffled but triumphant "YES!" emitted from the cupboard.

Hoping to humour him and distract him from carrying out any further electrical work, I said, "Oh well done, Mr Tyler. You were right, it was the fuse box. Now let's go and get your injection done so you can have your dinner. You must be exhausted after all that work today."

I checked his blood sugar level with a finger prick test

before taking the small glass vial from the fridge and drawing up the insulin into the orange-coloured syringe.

I could see he was restless and itching to get back to his work and – concerned for his safety – I tried to distract him by asking hopefully, "Are you going to leave the rewiring until tomorrow?"

"Oh, I expect so, nurse. Don't you worry about me. I know when I'm beaten for today."

I scanned the kitchen searching for some bread and made him a sandwich, choosing the slices of ham over the mouldy piece of cheese from the fridge. I wondered how much longer he could remain in his own home safely and decided to have a word with his GP to reassess him. Normally I would have stayed to chat and make sure he ate his supper, but this evening I just ensured he was sitting at his kitchen table with his sandwich and a cup of tea. Because of the weather I was more anxious to get on my way.

As I walked down Mr Tyler's path and glanced back at his house, I noticed all the lights had gone off again.

The next call was to a palliative care patient who lived with his anxious elderly wife. The Connors were a lovely couple and there was rarely anything practical to do there aside from checking he was comfortable and not in pain. We had learned from experience, an essential visit around this time of night would settle and reassure them both, and save us a call-out even later in the evening when we'd arrived back at base.

I had tried to delay going to Miss Johnson as long as possible, knowing she would not want to go to bed that early, but on leaving the Connors' house I was shocked to see a blizzard was fast covering my little white car and I was beginning to fear I might not get there at all.

I managed to clear as much snow as I could from the windscreen, every now and again rubbing my hands together briskly to shake the snow from my gloves, and jumped into the driver's seat with a shiver. I turned the key in the ignition and ... nothing ... aside from a pathetic splutter followed by a high-pitched squeaking noise. I desperately turned the key again in disbelief – still nothing.

Sitting for a minute, I tried to decide what to do next. There were no other cars around now, it was still snowing heavily, and the road was eerily silent. Trying and failing one last time to start my still uncooperative car, I remembered there was a telephone box in the next street and set off to walk there.

Walking down the middle of the deserted main road, the snow was teetering at the top of my knee-high boots and with every other step, I flinched at the cold shock when a little escaped over the top. Even trudging that short way was making me quite breathless and I could feel my heart pounding painfully as the cold air hit my lungs.

I was relieved to see the small slithers of remaining red of the telephone box in the distance and finally reaching it, I tugged hard on the heavy door – made more so by the snow that had accumulated at the base. It suddenly dawned on me I couldn't remember anyone's number so had no idea who I was going to call. It didn't seem urgent enough to call 999 for the emergency services. I thought of Miss Johnson waiting, and thinking I had no other choice, opted to try the ambulance depot. Surely they would be sympathetic and help me out? With a now painfully frozen index finger, I dialled 100 for the operator and asked to be put through to them.

"Hello, I wonder if you can help me. I'm one of the evening district nurses and my car has broken down."

"You must be joking, love. We're not coming out in this, not unless it's on a blue light anyway."

Sighing and using my shoulder to force open the heavy door again, and being several miles from base, I braced myself for the thirty-minute walk home with no option but to hope that Caroline would be able to call me or even have left a message on my home phone's answerphone.

After ten minutes of trekking and trying to recall the early symptoms of hypothermia and what I might do to prevent it setting in, I was starting to feel really scared. My mind dramatically picturing my frozen body being found in a snowdrift after days of being missing.

I thought I was hallucinating as I saw the headlights of the vehicle slowly ploughing its way towards me down the middle of the road. As it got closer, I could see it was the welcome sight of Caroline's Land Rover.

Almost in tears with relief, it was so good to see her welcoming smile as she opened the passenger door, beckoning me to climb in.

"Am I pleased to see you! How have you got on? I've still got Miss Johnson to do and my car is well and truly deceased."

"I'm done with my list so let's go to her together then I'll drop you home and we can sort your car out in the morning hopefully."

"You're early. I'm not ready for bed yet!" spat Miss Johnson.

I couldn't help myself. "Have you any idea what it's like out there?"

"Well there's two of you and the snow will grip your tyres, so I don't know what you're moaning about. In my day…"

We didn't wait to hear the next part. While I prepared the milk for her, Caroline – the braver of us and familiar with handling animals – fearlessly grabbed hold of the surprised Albert, popped him in his cage, and throwing in some seed, snapped shut the cage door.

"I'm still not going to bed yet. You just want to hurry me so you can get home – so thoughtless, you youngsters."

Caroline gave me a warning look which said, "Don't bite back" and interrupted her flow with, "What would you like to do, Miss Johnson? We really can't wait around or we'll both end up staying here for the night. There's no way we'll get home if we leave it much longer."

"Well, you'd better leave me in the chair then. I'll probably be warmer here anyway. It's what I used to do before you girls started interfering."

It didn't feel right but knowing we couldn't force her to go to bed we managed to find some extra blankets, a hot water bottle and a pillow from the bedroom and made her as comfortable as we could.

When we were back in the Land Rover, something felt amiss and I wriggled around uncomfortably in my seat for a while not wanting to sound rude or ungrateful for my very welcome lift, eventually getting the nerve to say, "I think I can feel something moving under here."

"Oh that's Charlie. He always comes round with me."

At the sound of his name, Charlie the cocker spaniel emerged from beneath my seat and lay down on my feet comfortingly, keeping them warm.

"I hope she'll be ok. She could have done with Charlie to keep her feet warm," I said, thinking of Miss Johnson.

"Oh, she's a tough old bird," Caroline replied, leaning forward to frantically scrape the ice from the inside of the windscreen and managing to make a small peephole.

We were just coming up to the warm and welcoming

lights of the 'The Fishers' when Caroline asked, "Is your babysitter staying the night?"

I pictured my babysitter, Angela.

"Yes, she'll probably be in bed frightening herself half to death watching a horror film by now."

We looked at each other and without needing to speak another word, Caroline turned sharply left into the pub carpark and minutes later we were sitting by the roaring fire in the huge brick fireplace enjoying a "Little tot of brandy on the house to warm you up," courtesy of Marg.

"We didn't think this night through very well, did we?" I pondered.

"We should have insisted on going round together in the Land Rover on a night like this. I can't believe the ambulance station don't see us as important enough to come out. They'd surely think differently if it was a male doctor who'd called on them."

Caroline agreed. "Yes, I think you're right. Let's bring it to our next team meeting with Mrs Hardy, and see what she suggests."

I nodded in agreement, although very much hoped it would be Caroline who 'did the bringing' to the intimidating Mrs Hardy.

After that dreadful snowy night and following yet another harrowing team meeting with Mrs Hardy, it had eventually been grudgingly agreed that the evening nurses – if they judged it a need – went around in pairs. This was a great advantage, both reassuring us about our safety and making the evening's work more enjoyable by having some company. The downside, however, was that we were often out later as fewer patients could be seen in the time, meaning an eleven o'clock finish regularly crept up to midnight.

The other innovative change was when two-way radios were introduced, which connected us directly to the ambulance depot. We were grateful that they agreed to take on the extra work this would have meant for them. The on-duty nurses would pick up the radios up from the base where they were on charge, returning them after their shift. Getting used to using the radios took some time.

Learning that it was not possible to speak and listen at the same time and other etiquette that the ambulance operatives were already familiar with was challenging at first for us. There was much embarrassment when it was realised that we needed to release the button on the side of the radio so the operator on the other end could not hear our private conversations, such as when we joked about the radio lingo: "Oooh, I wonder what 'Roger' looks like!".

The radios were somewhat a double-edged sword. They provided additional reassurance of our safety, but being 'two-way', the disadvantage was that GPs could contact us throughout the evening – sometimes to pass on the visits that would have been more appropriate for them.

Sarah picked up one of these calls when she and I were on duty one evening.

Mr Galloway

- A STORY OF CONSENT

It was New Year's Eve. We had returned to base and were just in the process of signing off for the evening. The radio beeped, its red light flashing, indicating we had a call. According to the ambulance operator (Geoff), the request came from an on-call GP who couldn't hide the background noise, suggesting he was already celebrating. Geoff said by the sound of the GP's slightly incoherent voice, "He was probably wise to stay put in any case."

Mr Galloway's wife had called the GP to say that her husband was having some sort of breakdown and was – as she spoke – throwing furniture around and completely out of control.

It was not the first time this had happened, although more recently his aggressive episodes had been well controlled by medication – until the previous day when he had refused to take it. Often an angry outburst stems from fear; although we never found out what, in his troubled mind, triggered Mr Galloway on that occasion. The danger to self and others is not to be taken lightly when a large man is out of control.

The psychiatrist could not visit until the following day and it was likely he was intending to section him (impose compulsory hospitalisation under the Mental Health Act) if he continued to refuse his medication, for his own and other's safety.

As midnight approached, all possibilities of our New Year celebrations slipped away from us. Afraid of what we were going to find, we held hands to calm ourselves as we walked cautiously up the path leading to Mr Galloway's house to administer the sedative injection that had been prescribed for him.

When Mrs Galloway opened the front door, she had clearly been crying.

Pointing to the small utility room off the hallway, she whispered, "I've locked him in there."

We'd never been called on to do anything like this before so we made a hurried plan that on reflection would have sounded like something from a comedy film if it hadn't been such a serious situation. Sarah would draw up the injection from the vial Mrs Galloway kept safely in the high kitchen cupboard for use in such circumstances. We would enter the room and I would talk to Mr Galloway to explain what we were to do, if necessary, holding his hands out of the way so that Sarah could find a spot on his thigh or buttock – whichever was the most easily accessible – and jab him.

With shaky hands, I slowly turned the key to the utility room and Sarah – looking like some sort of crazy doctor with her thumb ready on the plunger of the primed syringe held at face level – followed me in.

There was not too much damage in the room apart from a broken mirror, the shards of which crunched under our feet as we approached Mr Galloway, who was hunched in the corner of the room looking a lot more afraid than we were.

It turned out to be less difficult than we imagined, although I was very grateful that I wasn't on my own. Sarah administered the injection and he didn't resist, indicating his consent.

As the cuckoo clock in the hall mockingly called midnight, we helped him to bed. We stayed for a cup of tea – not quite the drink I was hoping for at New Year – with his very appreciative wife to be sure he had settled. When we peeked into his bedroom before we left, he was sleeping soundly.

Helen

- A STORY OF WORKING (AND PLAYING) TOGETHER

Like several of our patients, some of us had our own marital issues.

Helen, like me, had found herself a single mum of two boys about the same age as my girls. We enjoyed a friendship that extended beyond our work – our children also got on well. Although we had little money, we somehow scraped enough together to take them on a few days' holiday.

Even the constant rain in Blackpool couldn't dampen our spirits and determination to have fun. Donkey rides and fish and chips (mostly enjoyed by the kids, let's be honest!) and the fact we were all sharing a small room in a modest boarding house left us more exhausted than a typical workday.

As we both had to get babysitters when we were on duty, we sometimes liked to go out socially together after our shift if we didn't finish too late. On this particular evening, we were ever hopeful it might be an unusually quiet and uneventful. We optimistically had left our 'going-out' clothes back at base to exchange for our uniforms, and we were looking forward to a night out at a mutual friend's birthday party.

Even Miss Johnson had been surprisingly accommodating. It looked like there was a real possibility we could make it. Then … beep, beep, beep. The red light was flashing on the radio, meaning there was a message to be picked up from the ambulance depot.

It was a callout to Mrs Clarke, a lovely lady who lived in a warden-controlled flat and we knew she would not have called on us for no reason. She had a permanent catheter as her bladder – despite many different treatments over the years from the continence advisor and the urology consultant – was just not complying and emptying properly, which could have led to the serious situation of urinary retention and infections.

We knew from past experiences of visiting her that there was no point in trying to sort out why her catheter was not draining and that the entire catheter would need to be removed and a fresh one inserted. This is a procedure which can be challenging as trying to locate the opening to the female urethra can be a bit like threading a needle in the dark with one hand tied behind your back. To add to the difficulty, you are only allowed one attempt with each catheter tube, which then needs to be disposed of, trying again with a new one to reduce the possibility of infection entering the urinary tract.

From the moment we entered Mrs Clarke's home, our determination to enjoy a night out escalated. There was no need to speak to each other as we worked efficiently in perfect harmony, each having our own role. We washed our hands and donned our disposable gloves and Mrs Clarke, sadly (for her, but good for us) already familiar with the procedure, prepared herself on the bed ready for us to continue.

Helen opened the dressing pack and tipped the new catheter onto the sterile surface. I grasped it and with a deep breath aimed for the right spot. It was a difficult for us to resist a celebratory shout of BULLSEYE! but we didn't need to.

Mrs Clarke got in first with a smile, saying, "Thank you. That's the quickest yet. That was great; I didn't feel a thing. I'm glad I didn't hold you up too much. I expect you're really busy."

And indeed we were. Having completed our evening's work, we were busy planning to do what normal young women do on a Saturday night – CELEBRATE!

Thanks from the patients...

"Presents are made for the pleasure of who gives them, not the merits of who receives them."

Carlos Ruiz Zafón

An unspoken rule existed about us accepting gifts from patients and their families. A general guideline emerged: 'Refuse any gift more expensive than a tin of biscuits and receiving money is absolutely forbidden.'

Of course, these 'rules' didn't prevent many of our patients wanting to show their gratitude in this way, leaving us with a dilemma. We rarely considered refusing gifts as it would have been offensive.

Aside from the occasional box of chocolates (usually brought back to the nursing base for sharing) and Marg's delicious homemade cheese scones (which rarely made it further than my car), there were a number of other unique gift ideas.

Like the very expensive Royal Doulton Lady figurines a very well-off gentleman chose for us all in recognition for caring for his dying wife. Giving us each a beautifully wrapped box containing our gift, he had clearly put much thought into his choices, saying the delicate and beautiful figures reminded him of us on our visits. How could we refuse?

The wife of a man we were all very fond of, who had died after a long painful illness, was clearly not having any of our rules. She didn't directly offer us her monetary 'thanks' – knowing, I suspect, that we would have had to refuse. Instead, when each of us arrived home after visiting him during the last week of his life, we discovered she had secreted an envelope in the front pocket of our nursing bags. Each envelope containing a twenty pound note – an awful lot of money then.

It was tempting for me, given my limited income, to take the money, but of course it was not an option and we talked about what we should do at our next team meeting. We agreed we would donate it to a charity that supported people with the condition he died from.

At another monthly team meeting the secret of the success of green fingered Mr Lyttle's harvest of the tasty runner beans and tomatoes he regularly gifted to us was revealed. On a warm summer's evening, Sarah had gone out to his garden to say goodbye to him and spotted him emptying the urine from his wife's catheter bag onto the soil around his produce.

"It's the nitrogen that does it, nurse," he had told her with delighted excitement. "Much cheaper than buying fertilizer."

Our appreciation for home-grown vegetables took on a new meaning after that!

Then there was the gift that wasn't a gift at all. I

regularly visited a lady whose husband proudly showed me the bird tables, flower tubs and a variety of other garden ornaments he enjoyed making from pieces of scrap wood he had come across. They were reasonable efforts, and I quite liked the look of the bird tables. I could picture one in my small garden at home, and I knew my girls would love feeding the birds.

Every evening for the two weeks we visited his wife to renew dressings to a rather nasty infected mosquito bite to her leg – acquired when holidaying abroad with a friend. On the day of my final visit, he seemed even more pleased to show me his latest handiwork.

When he invited me out to his workshop, I was quite hopeful he maybe going to gift me a bird table, especially with all the interest I'd shown.

"Would you like this one, nurse? I know you said you liked it."

He pointed to the rickety looking bird table and then picked it up, offering it to me.

"Oh, are you sure? That's very kind of you."

"Of course, nurse. You've been very good to Irene. That will be fifteen pounds."

That was one gift I would have had no problem refusing as I could barely afford it, but it seemed I had no option. Silently cursing myself for being so enthusiastic about his work, I handed over the money and managed a smile somehow, getting it into my car with only a little bit sticking out of the side window. It didn't look too bad in my garden for the three weeks I had it before it fell apart.

By far the most memorable gifts were the ones we received at the 'award ceremony,' a festive drinks reception held at the Major's home each Christmas Eve morning. Although we weren't at work, it was not an option to refuse Mrs Kilpatrick's "11 a.m. prompt" summons.

We somehow felt obliged to wear our uniform as, along with the day nurses, we lined up in the huge sitting room – a glass of sherry in one hand, a Royal Albert porcelain tea plate with mince pie in the other – awaiting our presentation. Sarah (who didn't drink) managed to dispose of her sherry into the big potted Aspidistra in the corner without Mrs Kilpatrick noticing until she spotted her empty glass. Being the perfect host, to Sarah's dismay, she poured her another.

Our gifts were carefully selected by Mrs Kilpatrick. Some we had a suspicion, from their slight signs of wear, were possibly unwanted raffle prizes or donations from the charity shop where she volunteered on a Saturday.

Sarah – bottle of sherry.

Caroline – tea towel from Devon.

Helen – cushion with a picture of a dog.

Me – gold lamé evening bag.

Later, when we got together to unwrap them, it was clear that the gifts she had carefully chosen were based on her perception of us as being more like her, in taste and social standing, than we truly were. My gold lamé bag particularly caused us much amusement, although it was some time before I found the courage or the heart to regift it to a charity shop – one in another town just to be safe.

Yet, beneath the questionable choices, the act of giving gifts itself revealed something far more important: the significance of our role in the families' lives and the genuine appreciation they held for us.

Then and Now

"Nothing is more responsible for the good old days than a bad memory."

Franklin Pierce Adams

Things were changing in district nursing in the 1970s.

Nowadays, patients have more of a voice and more control over their treatment and some changes are clearly for the better and to protect the rights of the patient. For example, it would be unheard of now, and could even be considered a criminal act, to inject a patient without their expressed and clear consent.

Sadly, in those days there was less importance placed on the need to act quickly to treat the symptoms of a stroke. Had this knowledge been available then, people like the Major would have been offered almost immediately 'clot busting' drugs and therapies, enabling him to recover his mobility and speech more quickly.

There is less community spirit. Families are more divided geographically, with children moving away to the other side of the country for work. This means sick and especially older patients need more help from the dwindling overstretched statutory services if they want to remain in their own home.

Home Helps – similar to today's Home Care Workers – who often lived in the same street or at least nearby were more like friends to our patients and were allocated adequate time to spend with them – cooking nutritious meals, shopping keeping the house clean and generally looking after them. If a lightbulb needed changing or even a bit of gardening or decorating was required, their husbands were frequently around to step up and help.

Nurses and Home Helps were part of a team which included the family GP and social services. You could call the GP surgery in the morning and receive a home visit in the afternoon – yes, the same day! And the doctors knew their patients and their families and would bring a small envelope containing the patient's notes and medical history (now all electronic), and they would have time to sit with the patients and listen to their worries.

Treatments come and go: The use of maggots to clean wounds was well thought of in the 40s and 50s, frowned on after that (well, at least by me with Marge) and now back in fashion under the posh name of larvae therapy.

We rarely saw infections in our patients, even without today's hand gel, because we washed our hands regularly and thoroughly.

We seldom encountered patients who had pressure sores unless they had come from hospital or were extremely ill. We nursed them on sheepskin mattresses and turned frequently those who were confined to bed and could not move themselves (to relieve pressure – the main cause of skin breakdown). We cleansed, we massaged, we creamed vulnerable areas of skin to help improve the circulation.

Then pressure relieving mattresses and automatic beds came into fashion so we didn't need to touch our patients so much or visit so often.

No emails, no Google, no mobile phones, no long debates about the challenges of balancing safety with autonomy or paternalism. Just basic human care and meaningful contact.

We worried

… about our patients and their families:

The wife of a stroke patient who, having answered the door to us clearly very drunk, then got into her car and went for a drive around the countryside.

Or the man who had an oxygen cylinder in his bedroom and insisted on continuing to smoke forty cigarettes a day.

We cried

… for the patients we lost and for those whose suffering we couldn't ease.

We laughed – a lot!

…at the idea from a patient who was convinced a grape pip had come out of her eye.

…with a patient with MS who had just taken possession of a new electric bed that none of us could work out how to switch off. When the head and the foot of it worked together forming a V shape, he ended up sandwiched in the middle of it.

…when I asked the doctor (on behalf of a patient) if it was possible his amputated toe might grow back. (I'm still embarrassed about that!)

. . .

I'll leave it with you – the reader, to decide if these changes are all for the better.

About the Author

Alice went on to complete her specialist district nurse training when it became mandatory to do so in the 1980's

and eventually became a State Registered Nurse in the early '90s before leaving to take up another role as a respite care manager for people with MS and MND.

From her home in a North Lincolnshire village, Alice White – the dyslexic author who can spell – manages a busy psychotherapy practice alongside caring for a menagerie of pets.

This is her third book in the Reflections series of memoirs.

Follow Alice on Facebook:

AliceWhiteWriterAuthor

https://www.alicewhitewriter.co.uk

alicewhitewriter@outlook.com

... and Thanks from me

Thank you to the Evening Girls for the memories and team spirit I enjoyed with you during that twenty or so years. They will stay with me forever as some of the most difficult, emotionally charged and happy of my life.

Most of all, thank you to our patients and their families for teaching me so much about myself.

To this day, the smell of Palmolive soap makes me nauseous, and I can never go more than a couple of days without eating a cheese scone.

Printed in Great Britain
by Amazon

55041922R00069